GROWTH SPURTS

&

GROWIN' PAINS

THINGS I WISH I KNEW
VOLUME ONE

GORDON DOUGLAS

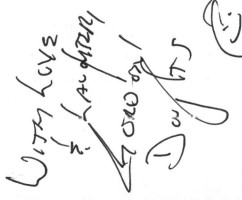

Published by CreateSpace, Charleston, SC

Edited by New Author Editing, Amsterdam, NY

Religious Nonfiction: *Growth Spurts & Growin' Pains: Things I Wish I Knew* by Gordon Douglas. Autobiographical material and jokes serve as a spiritual self-help guide.

ISBN 978-0-9987816-0-0

Library of Congress Control Number: 2017912845
Gordon Douglas Comedy Inc., Glen Mills, PA

About the Cover:

What the artist says about the cover art:

"The artwork for the cover of this book was done in watercolor, and in honor of Norman Rockwell, is a derivative work based on *The Bodybuilder*, a painting he did as magazine cover art. The idea is the same—the hopefulness that something, anything, would make the kid into a man. The pursuit of a dream of becoming someone else. I did this piece originally as a cover for one of Gordon's cassette tapes (remember cassettes?). The original has a title bar with the price and date to reflect this time in Gordon' life. All these years later, Gordon is still trying to beef up, to no avail."

About the Illustrator:

The artwork was done by Joy Kieffer. Joy is a personal friend of mine. Her work has been used by the Franklin Mint, Danbury Mint, Mannington Tiles, and the White House. For several years, she painted sports portraits, even though she has no interest in sports. But her work hangs in the homes of some very famous athletes, and their signatures are in hers.

She says to tell you that past work is just that—in the past. She still needs to eat, so she invites new opportunities. If you would like to see more of her work, or contact her, visit her at joykieffer.com.

She is also the author and illustrator of a series of garden journals (*The Garden Journal, Planner & Log Book*, etc., all available on Amazon). She uses these to help raise funds for the Giving Garden food pantry & garden housed at our church. She helps run the food pantry and garden, as well as and Lifewerks, Inc., a nonprofit that works with area schools, colleges, and other agencies to meet needs. Find out more about the garden journals and how you can help at gardenkitch.com.

ACKNOWLEDGMENTS

This whole book is really an acknowledgment of many, but not all (Volume Two is in the works) of the people who have been so helpful and instrumental in my life!

But special thanks to Mike Williams for hounding me to write this book for more than ten years, and for your great example in comedy, writing, and so much more.

Comedy legend, historian, and friend, Tommy Moore—thanks for your encouragement, your help with the editing, your input on many of the jokes from your vast library, and your knowledge of comedy.

To Joy Kieffer and our church that helps folks develop their gifts and beliefs in the arts (and for your primer on how to write this book that saved me countless hours).

Beth Brubaker, Kaitlyn Holmes, and Jennifer and Marc Manno for your extra editing and joke suggestions.

My wife, Dawn—I know you said this was my project, and you were extra busy during tax season, and you couldn't possibly take on another project, but... we are a team!

My brothers, Scott and Wade, whose knowledge of trivia and memories of our growing up is much better than mine. There, I said it.

To my whole family for allowing me to try new jokes, tell old jokes, and living with the clutter I leave on the dining room table each day. I know I have an office, but first, there is no room in there. It is messy. And second, I would miss all the daily fun. Who can work in that kind of quiet?

And to my special team of supporters who lift me up so blessings can come down. Thanks!

TABLE OF CONTENTS

PART I
THE WONDER YEARS

PART II
COMEDY CONNECTIONS

PART III
CROSS TRAINING

PART IV
READY TO LAUNCH

WARNING!

I have serious ADD issues and major short-term memory loss, and maybe long-term memory loss. This is my first book, so I'm not sure of my writing style, though I know I write like I talk. So, apologies to all the grammar Nazis out there. Sentences might be broken up, as this book is my life broken into thirty-plus stories. It's packed with hilarious jokes, meaningful quotes, and a game or two along the way. It includes things I've done right, things I've done wrong, and things I've screwed up. I hope you laugh and learn from some of the funniest situations I have found myself in while meeting some of the most amazing people that crossed my path as I traveled from Philly to Hollywood and thirty-eight states in between.

If you were sitting in my living room, or across from me at my favorite restaurant, Outback Steakhouse, this is how I would talk to you. Be warned—my wife says I have the gift of embellishment and exaggeration. So, at the expense of many laughs, great effort was made to make sure as many details as possible are as accurate as possible. Okay, that's a lie. Almost no effort was made. When I am telling the truth, and I think folks won't believe it, I say "really." Most quotes and jokes should be attributed to the right person. They really should, but that would require much more work than I am willing to give. And most are dead now, so the chances of being sued are slim.

For the record, we would be having a "blooming onion" if we ate at Outback. Well, I would be, and chances are I'd be hogging the special sauce (if a thought pops into my mind, I will try to use parentheses). Oh, and I'd order a rib eye, medium well, with the added side of crab legs. I'm not a big seafood person. Fish aren't really my thing. Except for the fish in *Finding Nemo*. What acting! Dorey was outstanding in her movie debut. The sequel is even better. I can't believe she memorized all those lines. Not bad for a young fish with short-term memory issues. I have short-term memory issues, and serious issues with ADD (not sure if I mentioned that). I have never been officially diagnosed with ADD. I did go online to take a test, but I quit. It was way too long. It was like—three questions. It would have, should have, confirmed that this is an issue for me. So, let's go. There is a lot of good stuff right around the corner. I believe that is true in this book and in your life. I want to help you find it!

INTRODUCTION

"I have spent a lot of time wondering why I am not happier..."
—David Letterman

"To jump or not to jump, that is the question." My toes inched closer to the edge. It was at least 400 feet to the bottom. From the small cliff I was perched on, the river looked like a piece of silver ribbon curling through the valley below. Questions swirled through my mind, as real as the breeze that blew through my hair. How did I get here? Why am I here? Do I really want to be here? If I died, would anyone miss me? How long would it take to hit bottom? But the biggest question on my mind was why would I pay $150 to zip line across a canyon? It has something to do with pleasing my daughter, Kristen, and my son-in-law, Buddy.

But there I was on the edge of a platform, built on the top of a slab of rock jutting out over an abyss. Of course, I had to go first. It's what dads do. Gotta make sure it's safe, and I am the comedian, which means if it isn't safe and I get hurt, I'll probably get a laugh. Fortunately, the wind kicked up, and the flapping of my pants hid the knocking of my knees. Our guide put me in some kind of medieval torture device with straps and buckles. He pulled extra tight on the belting, so my skinny excuses for legs could not, would not, slip. Could this get any worse?

You should never ever ask that question. Asking if things could get any worse seems to be a direct challenge to the unseen world. I found this out during my buckling-up procedure. A thick, heavy cloud moved in, making this 1500-foot zip line ride even more treacherous. You could no longer see across the canyon. Before, you could look down and see the tops of trees. Now, I could barely see the silhouettes of my family a few feet from me. Did I say from me? I meant behind me. I could hear them, though. "Come on, Dad, hurry up. They might not let us go if we wait any longer."

And so, with a deep breath and an affirmative nod from the team leader, I stepped off the platform and plunged into the unknown.

Maybe some of you reading this are there right now. Ready to take a leap of faith and leave your comfort zone. You know deep down in your heart that life has something more to offer. You have reached a point of "desperation." You are not sure where you're going or how to get there, but you know things

Yours truly, getting ready to take a giant leap, and inviting you to do the same with me in this book.

can't stay the same.

This book is for you. It's for anyone who wants more out of life. More Joy, More Miracles, More Challenges. As the funny philosopher, Yogi Berra, said, "If you don't know where you are going, you might wind up someplace else." Each of us has a unique path to take, but there are some things all journeys have in common, and that's why I want to invite you on a journey. My journey. After all, there are things we can all learn to make the trip more enjoyable and easier. Please learn from my mistakes; I've listed quite a few. I want you to avoid the dangers and delays. Experience delight, not disappointment.

So, are you ready to relive some key moments in my life? Ready to meet some of the funniest and most amazing people in the world? There is a very thin line between comedy and tragedy, and you will laugh as I share some of the weird predicaments I have been in, and some of my favorite jokes. And it might be good to have a tissue box handy, just in case... you know, allergies kick in. They seem to get worse when you are around someone who shares their heart.

Chinese philosopher Lao Tzu, a contemporary of Confucius, said, "The journey of a thousand miles begins with a single step." It's time to take that step. Or maybe it's a plunge. Either way, buckle up, turn the page, and get ready for a rollercoaster ride of ups and downs, twists and turns, tickles and truths. Get ready to see your life change.

"If you want to be successful, you have to jump. There is no way around it. When you jump, I can assure you that your parachute will not open right away. But if you do not jump, your parachute will never open. If you are safe, you will never soar."
—Steve Harvey

PART I

THE WONDER YEARS

CHAPTER 1
BEAUTY & THE BEAST

"I entered a beauty pageant once. Really. Of course, I finished last, but I got 461 get well cards."—Phyllis Diller

So, this guy works for the circus. His job is to follow the elephant with a broom and a shovel. His friend says, "That's a horrible job. Why don't you quit?" and the guy says, "What, and give up show business?"—From the Files of Tommy Moore

"Dammit, Jim, I'm a doctor, not an escalator!"—Dr. McCoy on *Star Trek*

The first step of my journey was down. Getting off the escalator in the Tampa International Airport, my heart skipped a beat. A handsome black man, wearing a very distinguished uniform, held a sign with my name on it. There was usually a line of them right next to baggage claim—a row of well-dressed men, holding signs with someone's name on them. The contract said that someone was supposed to pick me up, but this was a real surprise. Usually it was a guy in a beat-up car, but never a limo driver. After thirty years, my comedy career was taking off. Welcome to the big time!

I went over and introduced myself, and we headed for baggage claim. Having ADD, I hate to wait. The longest time period of any trip is waiting for your suitcase to come out that little chute. Mine was bright orange with a large rubber band on the zipper. This makes it easy to tell my suitcase from the others, and the rubber band helps find which of the three zippers actually opens the suitcase. Polite small talk took place as our eyes remained glued to the conveyor belt as it went around. It's not as exciting as childbirth, but close. There's a rush that comes when you see that sweet suitcase tumble down the little slide and come toward you. I reached to snag my bag before it could race by me.

"DO NOT TOUCH THAT BAG, SIR!" barked my driver, who now positioned himself properly to do the "grab, swing, and pivot" maneuver. This is necessary to hoist my forty-nine-pound suitcase and place it on the floor without throwing your back out. My wife is a savant when it comes to packing as much as possible without going over the fifty-pound limit. My driver was apparently a savant at picking up suitcase. That former military man didn't even grunt. I risked a hernia.

"Follow me!" came a command as he double-timed it toward the doors to the outside. We didn't go to the parking garage—we went outside to what looked like a runway for small planes. Apparently, the double-stretch limousine can't make the turns in a parking garage. Who knew?

Yes, you heard right—a double-stretch limo, all cleaned and polished, waited for me. This beats the VW bus I've been driving for the last fifteen years. My old buggy hadn't seen a car wash in over a decade. A person could live for a year from the Cheerios and assorted snacks on the floor. This limo had a bar; my lime-green ride had half-filled juice boxes scattered about. A huge grin spread across my face as I looked at this classy ride.

As I reached for the door latch, the words, "DO NOT TOUCH MY CAR, SIR!" caused me to flinch and step back. My driver (you gotta love the sound of that—"my driver") squeezed by me and opened the door for me to enter. This is not a car you get in. You must "enter." The lights, the phone, the TV, the fancy wine glasses lit up the room. My kids could play hide and seek in there.

After joining me in the back, he gave a tutorial on how to use everything. "How long will we be driving?" I asked the driver. Sorry, I meant my driver. It was going to be close to a two-hour ride. My next question stunned him. "Would you mind if I rode up front with you?"

He replied with Southern dignity. "Well, sir, I've been

driving nigh on ten years, and no one has ever asked me that, but I would enjoy some company if you would like to come up front."

This former Navy SEAL told me he had trouble adjusting when he came home from the war. It cost him his marriage, and though fishing every day from the pier of your beach home sounds ideal, it got boring. Time flew quickly as we flew down the interstate. We chatted about all kinds of things, but mostly his time in the Middle East.

"We are getting close to the hotel. Is there anything you want to see or do before we get there?" he asked.

"Could we stop at McDonald's? My wife gave me a coupon, and it would be cool to go to the drive-thru in a limo with a coupon!"

He laughed, but I was serious. "No, sir, we can't do McDonald's. This limo is too long to get around the turn!"

When we got to the hotel, people in the lobby gawked at me as my driver opened my door. "Who is it?" one patron said in a rather loud whisper.

Crossing the lobby, my mom's voice echoed in my head. "Look like you've done this before!" Folks paused and stared at my bright orange suitcase being hauled out of the trunk. Then they paused and stared as I walked to the main desk. You could see the confusion on their faces, as they debated if they should rush over and get an autograph. I looked important, wearing my suit on the plane. Something a veteran comedian taught me—in the event your baggage is lost, you're ready to go!

The conference room was elegant. This was a big-time event. It was a huge gala for a Catholic charity raising money to help girls in an unexpected, or unplanned, pregnancy. Major League Baseball players were there; NFL football players were there. Even an ice sculpture was there— something you don't see in the comedy clubs or VFW posts where I normally perform.

Best of all, sitting next to me at the head table, was Miss America. She was stunning. Her smile lit up the room. Folks came over to get her autograph and take pictures. This was before cell phones with cameras, and long before the invention of the "selfie." So, it became my job to take someone's camera and snap a picture. One picture per camera. Don't want to waste film!

As she chatted with her admirers, an announcement was made that the chocolate fountain was closing soon. That was all I needed to hear. I boogied over and loaded up a plate of strawberries, marshmallows, and pretzels, all smothered in brown liquid magic. As we were encouraged to take our seats, I placed the plate between us, telling Miss A. (we were now using first initials) to help herself. She touched my arm, and with a heavy Alabama accent, said, "Aren't you soooo sweet!"

The dinner was amazing, and soon I was on stage doing my fifteen-minute warm-up act to a very responsive audience. There were huge laughs, and applause filled the room (and my head). What a night! Folks were now asking for my autograph and wanting to take a picture with me. "Oh, Miss America, would you be a dear and take a picture of us?"

Next thing you know, it's morning, and I'm standing at the baggage claim in Philadelphia, alone. When I saw my orange suitcase arrive, I called my wife waiting in the cell phone lot so we could make a quick exit. My huge grin from the last twenty-four hours was still there.

My wife pulled up in our green VW bus. She watched me stand on the curb, where I hesitated for just a second to see if she wouldn't mind loading my bag or opening the sliding door for me. It didn't happen. Nope. Instead, as soon as I got in and before I could buckle my seatbelt, my wife said, "The school called this morning." The school is CADES—the Children and Adult Disability Educational Services, formally known as Cerebral Palsy of Delaware County. It's where I've worked since 1983 as the part-time maintenance man. I normally tell folks I'm the head of maintenance, which is true. The fact that I am also the only maintenance man is also true.

Dawn's stare was intense, and she clenched the steering wheel hard. Her eyes darted left and right, like Clint Eastwood in a gunfight, as she eased away from the curb. She hates driving in the city, and the airport buses and folks in a hurry scare her. "Let's stop on the way home!" I said. "They never see me in a suit."

When we arrived at the school, the reaction as I walked in

was what I hoped for. "Look at you in a suit. Did someone die?" Catcalls and whistles followed me everywhere. I went to the receptionist and said, "My wife said you called this morning. Something need fixing?"

"Yes," she said without a smile. "The toilet in Room 8 is overflowing!"

"Really?"

"Really!"

With a plunger in one hand, and holding my tie back with the other, I attacked the problem. Welcome to my world. The good and the bad, the highs and the lows. In twenty-four hours, I went from the red carpet to the red plunger. Maybe this chapter could be called "The Princess and the Plunger".

I WISH I KNEW

"People like to cherry pick the parts of their career that they are in the midst of, or that they are most proud of. But the truth is, careers and lives are tapestries."—Mike Rowe, star of *Somebody's Gotta Do It*

As we end each chapter, I want to share something I WISH I KNEW, and maybe give you something to do to help you know where you are, who you are, where you're going, or some practical advice on meeting your goal. I wish I knew that I am not defined by what I do. It shouldn't matter whether I have a microphone in my hand or a plunger, or whether I'm entertaining 2,000 people in a convention center or fixing the wheelchair of someone without insurance—my life has value. Your life has value. Happy people know that what they do makes a difference.

Quick story. Three men are laying bricks. They are asked, "What are you doing?" The first guy, wiping his sweaty brow, says, "I am laying bricks." Second man, standing a bit taller, answers, "I am making a wall." The third guy says with a smile, "I am building a hospital where thousands will come and get better." See the difference? They are all doing the same thing, but with a different perspective. So, how would you answer, "Who are you? What are you doing? Do you feel good about what you are doing? How is it making a difference?"

Keep reading, and let's find out what you want to do!

CHAPTER 2
LET'S TALK ABOUT SEX!

A little boy asks his grandma, "How old are you?" Grandma answers "You should never ask a woman her age." The little boy asks, "Well, then, how much do you weigh?" She says a bit sternly, "Oh, that is even worse. A gentleman never asks a woman her weight!" The little boy leaves, and then comes back a few minutes later with Grandma's purse. "Grandma, I found your purse and saw your driver's license and found out everything I wanted to know. You are 81 years old, you weigh 187 pounds, and you got an F in Sex!"—From the Files of Tommy Moore

"I remember when the air was clean and sex was dirty!"—George Burns

"I don't watch a lot of TV anymore. A lot of it isn't the kind of thing you can feel comfortable with watching with your kids. And I still feel that way, even though, now, my kids are in their thirties."—Tim Conway

The word SEX was written in eighteen-inch letters on the blackboard. It certainly got my attention, and the attention of the folks who entered this workshop at a healing conference. I am not sure what people are more interested in: Sex or Healing. In my show, I often ask, "Who invented sex? It was not somebody named Victoria who can't keep a secret!" But my interest in healing is huge, due to the deep emotional hurt that most folks, including me, carry around. My world is filled with folks dealing with physical and mental problems. So, sitting in our chairs in a packed room, we stared at the three letters that caused many of us to question sitting down. Breathing changed as an uncomfortable atmosphere swept the room.

The special guest arrived, smartly dressed in dress pants and jacket, no tie. Professional, yet not stuffy. With a big smile, he looked at the letters on the board, and then at us. "Anyone think they are in the wrong conference?" he asked with a twinkle in his eye. He got a polite chuckle in response, and a few people started to put their notebooks away and get ready to dart for the door.

"Today, I want to talk about S-E-X!" he declared, spelling out each letter. "S-E-X. That stands for Significant Emotional Experiences." (Okay, "Experiences" doesn't start with X, but it has the letter x in it. Besides, the word SEE wouldn't have made so many of us uncomfortable.) What a great attention-getter. This is going to be fun.

"Each of you has a piece of yellow tablet paper. Take out a pen and write down the ten worst things that ever happened to you. Maybe write down a few names of folks who hurt you, lied to you, betrayed you, stole from you, or abused you."

TEN? I thought to myself. *I could fill both sides of this piece of paper.* And I did, and it was not fun. Just thinking about certain people or events caused me pain. Through tear-filled eyes, I saw a big picture of an iceberg on the screen. This was long before PowerPoint. Our guest speaker continued. "Most of us are like icebergs. What people see is just a portion above the surface of the water, but most of us have a lot more going on beneath the surface."

These Significant Emotional Experiences need to be dealt with to be healed. To ignore them is like trying to push a beach ball under water—it keeps popping back up. Your hurts will come to the surface again and again. The hurts help form who we are, and what we respond to. It is not the purpose of this book to take you through all that I learned about healing, but there will be some steps to help you in this book. The Appendix has some great resources to take you deeper.

To write this book, I looked back, trying to connect the dots of how I got to be who I am and why I do what I do. Right now, in front of me, is a board filled with Post-It notes. Twenty of the best things that ever happened to me. Names of people who helped me, or had a great influence on me. The ten funniest things I've ever said or done, and, yes, some of the worst things that have ever happened to me. Looking back over my sixty years, there have been a lot more than ten in each category. In fact, there are at least three more *Things I Wish I Knew* books being birthed from this SEX thing. (Get it? Being birthed?) This one is all about my Growin' Pains and Growth Spurts.

Reflecting on many of these events brings such joy to my heart. Faces of folks I am indebted to and grateful for flash through my mind and I can't help but smile. You'll find out why on the following pages. And yes, more than a few tears have been shed as I relive some of the difficult and painful times in my life. Some I have caused; some I was a victim. So, both are included—some of the happiest and best things in my life, along with the people who had such a great impact on my life for good, and some of the terrible times and what got me through them.

I WISH I KNEW

Princess Buttercup: You mock my pain!
Dread Pirate Roberts: Life is pain, Highness. Anyone who says different is selling something.
Princess Buttercup: You mocked me once. Never do it again. I died that day!
—From *The Princess Bride*

Most comedians I know have had some great tragedy in their life. In fact, it's not just comedians, but most people I know. I wish I knew that ignoring, hiding, and burying my pain would have such a profound impact on my life, affecting how I feel about myself, and how I see the world. I wish I knew that healing was available, and that there is something you can do today to bring some instant relief, and other things that will get you started on the road to recovery! But you can begin by identifying and admitting your hurts.

"You can't connect the dots looking forward; you can only connect them looking backwards. So, you have to trust that the dots will somehow connect in your future. You have to trust in something—your gut, destiny, life, karma, whatever."—Steve Jobs

CHAPTER 3
I WAS AN ADDICT AT THIRTEEN

"Why would I spend $2,000 on braces for a teenager who never smiles?"—Erma Bombeck

"When a child turns twelve, he should be kept in a barrel and fed through the bung hole, until he reaches sixteen... at which time you plug the bung hole."—Mark Twain

"Nowhere in the Bible does it say how old Lucifer was when he rebelled against God. My guess would be fifteen!"—Jeff Allen

My mom kept saying, "These are the best years of your life!" What a lie. I hated becoming a teenager. Until, one day, I discovered something. I couldn't believe anything could feel so good. I was hooked. At thirteen years of age—which is young, very young—to experience this kind of euphoria for the first time. We had moved the year before from a small town named Lester, just outside the Philly Airport. In fact, my great-grandmother's house was literally the first house you see at the end of the runway. It made her angry when they expanded I-95 and lengthened the runway because she had a little "still" back in the swamps of Tinicum that made some homemade "medicine."

Gram Shoppee had a strong accent and a stronger personality. She came to this country in 1897 and lived to be ninety-two. Family stories talk of her stowing away on a boat as a fifteen-year-old. She and a few of her fifteen siblings escaped from a revolution on the Russian/Prussian border. Names of countries changed often depending on who had the best army.

Most of our family lived within a few blocks of each other, and most worked at the Westinghouse plant, or the Lester piano factory. It was a very ethnic neighborhood. Our neighbors were the Battistas, the Pepes, the Rubellas, the Yanivinchiaks. My dad's mother came from Scotland in 1927 looking for work, just before the Depression. Grandmom Douglas lived across the street. Her neighbor, Nellie, was from Russia, and had a big German shepherd named Gustof. You didn't mess with Nellie, or Gustof. Family and friends were in a small community. It was home.

But in 1966, my parents bought land in the country, and aunts and uncles pitched in and built us a house on an old

Christmas tree farm. It was a full half hour outside the city, in the farms of Glen Mills. There were new challenges. It wasn't like boarding a boat with your life's possessions in a few boxes, or learning a new language, or building a new life in a new land, but it was a big change for me. I even changed my name. Most of my family calls me by my middle name, Glenn, because my dad was Gordon. But in a new school, with a new start and first and last names on the attendance sheet, I became Gordon. Not that I minded. Like every boy, I wanted to be like my dad.

In the '60s, many families made the move from the city to the suburbs. My relatives said we were moving to "the country." Farms became developments, and as the population grew, a new school was built: Garnet Valley Junior/Senior High School. When our sports teams went to "away" games, people would sing *Farmer in the Dell*, or make "mooing" sounds like a cow. Classic Philly trash talk. Attendance was about 600 students, grades 7-12. It was small school, but a big adjustment.

And like everyone else, I craved attention. Maybe a little more than most. Is that nature or nurture? Who knows. Most of us want to fit in, and cliques are fairly well formed by that age. There were the jocks, and the good-looking kids, and the smart kids. I was "none of the above." And, of course, there was the "rough crowd" who smoked in the bathroom between classes. You learned to hold your bladder and bowels to avoid the smoke and being bullied. More than once I was tied to a book rack, or hung over a toilet to get a "swirlie."

Every now and then the school had an assembly. The whole student body would gather in the auditorium to watch a movie, learn the dangers of drunk driving, or listen to the chorus and band during the holidays.

It was during one of those assemblies that my life changed. Some science guy came in. A long line of students entered the auditorium in the lower hall by the music room. Seems like the principal always carried a paddle (is that true, or just a bad memory?). As we walked by, he motioned for a few of us to get out of line. He then took us backstage. There, in the dark, with no one watching, it happened.

This "Bill Nye the Science Guy" type came over and gave us stuff and whispered, "Don't say anything." This was very suspicious, but I didn't have much time to think about it because a minute later, the show started. He told a few stories and did a few experiments involving several students from backstage. The flashes of fire and color-changing liquids had us "country bumpkins" impressed.

Then he told a story of a notorious jewel thief who had recently escaped with a famous diamond. The thief was rumored to be in our area. In fact, he was last seen running into this very school. The hushed crowd glanced around looking for a guilty face. "There is a special machine that can identify the thief," he said, pulling out a little machine with a wand. He waved it over each of us on stage. When he got to me, it began to chirp.

17

He walked away and it stopped, and so did he. Dramatically, he stared at the machine to see what was wrong. Taking advantage of the lull, I made a face, and the crowd giggled. Slowly, he turned and came back to me. The chirping beginning again. He stopped and faced the audience to make sure they could see the progress being made in solving this diamond caper.

And as he turned away, I shrugged my shoulders, put my hands up, and made a "WHO ME?" face, making the crowd laugh. He looked back at me, but by now I was standing still and looking solemn. The chirping sound increased in speed and volume as he pointed the wand at my pants pocket. At which point, following his whispered instructions, I reached in my pocket and returned the rock he had given me earlier. That year, Barbra Streisand won an Oscar for best actress in *Funny Girl*, but my silent look of guilt and shame should have won me the Oscar as "Funny Guy".

Walking offstage, I gave a grin and a little wink to the crowd, pointing to my pocket like I still had something he missed. And they roared. The next few days, people in the hallways would smile and point at me. "That's the funny kid from the stage!" Upperclassmen looked at me. I was SOMEBODY because of laughter. That moment set the stage for the rest of my life (pun intended). The feelings that came with the laughter were tied to my heart's longing to be accepted and do something special. And this felt good, really good. I was hooked.

Chuckie Lewis (right) and me during our formative years.

I WISH I KNEW

"The one thing you think you can do better than everyone else—go out and do that. The light shining out of your eyes should blind people."—Garrett Oliver

I wish I knew there was something I would be good at. I spent so much time as a kid wishing I could be someone else, or have someone else's looks or talent. How would you answer the question, "If you could get a million dollars a year to do anything in the world, what would it be?" Deep down, we all have dreams and desires. You don't have to be better than everyone else. Just think, "What do I enjoy doing most?" Is there a career or field related to that?

One of my favorite jokes is "We have twenty-three kids. One of each!"

"I can live for two months on a compliment!"—Mark Twain

The audience will sit and stare until it hits them—we are all different. Twenty-three kids? One of each?? Yes, there is a loud one, a quiet one, a neat one, a sloppy one, a musical one, an athletic one, a determined one, a laidback one… Each with distinct talents, personalities, and great potential. My Uncle Bill was an electrician from South Philly. He loved his job. He once told me, "You are going to work the rest of your life. Find something you like!" Great advice.

I wish I would have listened.

CHAPTER 4
FANNING THE FLAME

"I find that a duck's opinion of me is highly dependent on whether or not I have bread."—Mitch Hedberg

"When I went to school, all I had was a pencil. And the kid next to me... if he had applied himself, I could've been somebody!"
—Gene Perret

"The number one quality for success is sincerity. There is nothing better, and the sooner you can fake it, the better off you will be."
—George Burns

Little Tommie was asked, "What do you want to be when you grow up?" "I want to be a preacher!" "Oh, Tommie, that is wonderful. Why do you want to be a preacher?" "I figure if I have to go to church, it will be more fun to stand up and yell than sit down and listen."

I grew up going to church. Most families in the '60s did. After we moved, we ended up at Stonybank Community Church, so named because it was just down the road from a quarry. A small church that looked like something out of *Little House on the Prairie*, it has a small cemetery with dates going back to the early 1700's. Our church had forty to fifty folks most Sundays, sitting on rock-hard pews with straight backs. One day, our little church got a new pastor, Pastor Bill Neff. And he was under 100, which I thought was the minimum age for pastors. Pastor Bill invited me to ride with him to the Sandy Cove Conference, right on the Chesapeake Bay in Maryland.

I had never been in a car with a pastor. What music would he put on the radio? Would he pray, or quote Scripture? It was a nice ride through farms, past the world-famous Longwood Gardens. Getting off Route 1 in Nottingham, you can smell the potato chips being made in the Herr's factory. You can actually take a tour there and watch them being made, and they even bring you samples right off the conveyor belt. Heaven on earth!

Spending time with a new pastor was a new experience for me. No one I knew had ever done that before. He seemed interested in me, and he had a great laugh. This pastor was… how do I put it? Human.

When we arrived at Sandy Cove, the view of the Chesapeake was awesome. And a huge crowd of more than 500 folks crammed into the big field house. After some robust singing of classic camp music, we listened to a young gal sing a new song, *My Tribute (To God Be the Glory)* by Andraé Crouch. And she got a standing ovation and shouts of "Encore!! Encore!!" After catching her breath, she sang it again, word for word, note for note. Ending long and strong and bringing the audience to their feet again!

As the crowd slowly took their seats, her dad, Don Lonie, was introduced. I had never heard of Don Lonie, but apparently, after speaking at 300 schools a year for ten years, a lot of folks had. And they were eager to hear his unique mix of stand-up comedy and inspiration. He was hilarious, his act was clean, and I had a blast hanging out with a pastor.

Going home was like floating on a cloud. I couldn't imagine anything better on earth. Until we stopped for an ice cream cone. My family was cheap. Dirt cheap. We rarely ever stopped for something like ice cream. "Why pay one dollar to buy a cone when you can get a half-gallon for $3.99?" my mom would say. My Scottish dad would tell us, "If the ice cream truck is ringing the bell, it means he's out of ice cream." We'd sit on the porch on most summer nights, waiting for the truck to come by, but he was always ringing that bell. He always seemed to run out before he made it to our house." Okay, that's an old joke, but it isn't far from the truth.

So, here I was with Pastor Bill, holding an ice cream cone, smiling as wide as a young boy can. But the event was quickly forgotten, or at least buried. Family vacations, sports, school took its place. Life goes on, I guess. But the seed was planted, and a small root began to form. If there is anything better then laughing, it is helping others laugh. At least for me.

I WISH I KNEW

"We are lending money that we don't have to kids that will never be able to pay it back, to educate them for jobs that no longer exist. That's Nuts!" —Mike Rowe

I wish I knew that I would be happiest doing something I love. I know my boys all wanted to be Michael Jordan when they were thirteen. What little kid doesn't dream of adventure? My comedy buddy, Dave Hopping, said, "When asked in kindergarten what we wanted to be, some kids said I want to be a fireman, or astronaut. Others said doctors and lawyers. When the teacher asked me, I said, 'I want to be a kangaroo.'" But that is Dave. When my girls were growing up, one wanted to work with animals, another wanted to solve crimes like the detective in *Monk*. And they loved the show *Psych*. Television can plant seeds, too. Can you think of what you wanted to be or do before you were ten, or during your teen years? Did it change after high school? Are you doing anything now that relates to your dream as a teenager? Did anything happen to encourage you to pursue your dream?

CHAPTER 5
MY DAD WAS A
HEADCASE

Doctor: I'm sorry, but I have some bad news.
Patient: How long do I have, doctor?
Doctor: 10!
Patient: 10 what? 10 years, 10 months, 10 weeks...
Doctor: 9-8-7...

"You know my doctor, Dr. Vinny Boombatz. The other day I said, 'Doctor, every morning when I get up and look in the mirror, I feel like throwing up, What's wrong with me?' He said, 'I don't know, but your eyesight is perfect.'"—Rodney Dangerfield

From the TV show *M*A*S*H*:
"Oh, go salute yourselves!"—Margaret "Hot Lips" Houlihan

"The way I see it, the army owes us enough coffee breaks, we can take 1954 off!"—Hawkeye Pierce

"Dear Mom: As usual I am writing slowly, because I know you can't read fast."—Radar O'Reilly

"I am going to live through this, even if it kills me!"—Corporal Max Klinger

"I want foxholes there, there, there, and there, each one smartly dug. The kind of hole a man can throw himself into with pride."—Frank Burns

"Cow Cookies! Horse Hockey! Holy Hemostat! Jumping Jehoshaphat! Busload of Bushwah! Mule Muffins! Hell's Bells! Monkey Muffins! Pigeon Pellets! Beaver Biscuits!"—Colonel Harry Potter

There were no remote controls to the television in our day. My brother was the remote control, and my dad gave him a nudge on the back of his head from his throne of a chair, with the command, "Go change the channel." I would have done it, but I was just the right size to hold the rabbit ears and touch the screen at the same time to get rid of most of the snow on the picture. Snow was only one problem—the rolling picture was another. But my dad never let anyone touch the buttons on the back or in the secret compartment, 'cause you didn't know what might happen.

We had no cell phones in those days, either. Just one phone, on the wall in the kitchen, right by the door to the garage. "Go answer the phone!" my dad barked. In those days, it was a big deal to answer the phone. There was normally a race to see which kid would get there first. But no one was running tonight, because the phone wasn't ringing.

Something wasn't right with my dad. He and I had put the snow tires on the Malibu wagon that afternoon. I loved helping my dad work on the car. "Dam Sam and son of a gun!" was his way of cussing when something didn't go right, like hitting his finger with the wrench, or hitting his head on the car, both of which he did that day.

He was squatting like a baseball catcher, lifting the tire, while trying to line up the holes on the rim with the bolts on the wheel. Somehow, he lost his balance, and not wanting to drop the tire or hit the jack, he hit his head on the side of the car. A shake of his head and a little rub, and all seemed fine. No big deal. My dad was big and strong and fast. He looked a lot like Christopher Reeve in the first *Superman* movie. And to me, he was Superman.

He served in Korea as part of the medical corps in a MASH hospital. He didn't talk about it—ever. A few weeks before my mom's passing, she shared a few stories, like the week he came home from the war when a car barreling down the street backfired. He jumped on my mom to protect her and broke the bed. She said his job was to drive the ambulance into enemy territory, get the wounded soldiers, and bring them back to

My dad in uniform. Like I said, Superman.

the MASH unit. It changed him. Most pictures of him before the war, he was smiling, but after the war, not so much.

In high school, he was a tremendous athlete, holding a state record in the javelin. He did the high jump, leaping over six feet into a sawdust pit (no big cushions in those days). Which just reminded me of a joke. "The East German pole vaulter became the west German pole vaulter today." (Thanks George Carlin!) Back to my dad, whose nickname was Scotty. He played semi-pro football for the Aston Knights, but his greatest sport was baseball. When he stole a base, he always dove into second base like Pete Rose. He loved Charlie Hustle because he played the game "the way it was supposed to be played"— with passion.

Before leaving for Korea, he pitched back-to-back shutouts on the same day. It is still some kind of record because his name was recently in the newspaper again. You know the section that has headlines and top stories from days gone by… 10, 20, 30, 40, and 50 Years Ago Today? And there was his name, still getting more press than me. So, a little bump on the head was no big story.

The trip to the doctor's on Monday led to some tests and X-rays on Tuesday. The pictures showed a tiny brain tumor the size of a pea behind his ear. A follow-up visit a week later revealed it had grown to the size of a lemon. Emergency surgery was needed, and needed now. My mom was crying, something she never did. But I wasn't worried. I had seen Chad Everett in *Medical Center* on TV. They had a similar case where they diagnosed and fixed a brain tumor before the one-hour show was over. By the end of the show, everyone was smiling, including Chad.

Brain surgery and heart surgery weren't anything like today. Medicine had come a long way from leeches and blood-letting, but this was the early 1970's, and there was still a whole lot to learn, particularly about the brain. There are several great hospitals in Philadelphia—even world-renowned—including the University of Pennsylvania Hospital. It was one of those hospitals—one of the best in the country—that eventually took his case.

This sixteen-year-old me was not prepared for what I saw after driving my mom back to the hospital in our bright orange VW bug. She had come home after his all-day surgery to get a few hours of sleep. The sight of my dad lying in a bed with a shaved head stunned me. There was a huge scar where they lifted off his skull, and tubes all over his body, with more wires going into his head then there were in the back of our TV.

Pain management was minimal, as they wanted to "monitor his brain activity." For days, we sat there and listened to him groan. He rarely opened his eyes. I can't imagine the horror he felt, as more than once he begged me to get him a gun. I didn't think anything could hurt so bad as seeing your hero so weak, helpless, and desperate. For several weeks, nothing seemed to change, until the phone rang again. For the first time since I could remember, no one raced to answer it. My brother and I didn't fight over it. It was as if we knew there was finally a change, but not for the good.

I answered the phone, where a nurse screamed that they needed help with my dad. Something about him being restrained. Finding my mom was hard before cell phones. It was almost an hour later when she finally came home from getting some groceries. After a quick update and a call to the hospital, we jumped in the car and raced back into the city.

It was Halloween, and the rooms were filled with decorations of ghosts, witches, and other evil-looking things. Very scary stuff for someone who is medicated. To make matters worse, many of the nurses were Asian. As my dad regained consciousness, between the brain surgery and the meds, he thought he was back in the war, and he did what any soldier would do—he fought off the enemy.

The man I grew up believing could do anything now lay on a bed with leather straps on his arms and feet, tubes and wires running everywhere. To see him this weak and helpless was more than I could bear. As my mom held his hand, I walked out and to the end of the hall and just sobbed. It didn't end like TV. There were no smiling doctors waving as he exited the hospital with a triumphant smile and wave of his hand. It wasn't an hour before he came home. It was close to two months before he left the hospital and could sleep in his own bed. The God I believed was always there seemed nowhere to be found. If God was there, He didn't seem to care. And if God wouldn't help me or my father now that we needed Him most, I wanted nothing to do with Him.

I WISH I KNEW

"When people are like, Life is good, I go, No, life is a series of disastrous moments, painful moments, unexpected moments, and things that will break your heart. And in between those moments, that's when you savor, savor, savor."—Sandra Bullock

I wish I knew that every day is a gift, and that life as we know it can change in a moment. Older folks remember the attack on Pearl Harbor, and many of us can still see the planes crashing into the towers on September 11th. National tragedies that changed a country, but what about personal tragedy? Most of us have had our own personal traumas, and we will talk more about healing later, but for today... if you only had today, or a month, or a year left, what would you do? Who would you talk to, or spend time with? What would you say? Got something or someone in mind? Why wait?

Oh, one more thing. It is natural to look for someone, or something, to blame. We all do it. It's part of the grieving process. Julie Axelrod wrote that "The 5 stages of grief and loss are: 1. Denial and isolation; 2. Anger; 3. Bargaining; 4. Depression; 5. Acceptance. People who are grieving do not necessarily go through the stages in the same order or experience all of them." So, who do we blame? God is an easy target. If God is all powerful and all loving, why do such bad things happen? It's a good question—one that we will not ignore but touch on throughout the book and the next volume. But at that stage of my life. I was angry and hurt,

5 STAGES OF GRIEF
1. Denial
2. Anger
3. Bargaining
4. Depression
5. Acceptance

confused and disappointed in whatever God is out there.

"...just because I (the LORD) work incredible good out of tragedies doesn't mean I orchestrate the tragedies. Don't ever assume that My using something means I caused it or need it to accomplish My purposes. That will only lead you to false notions about Me. Grace doesn't depend on suffering to exist, but where there is suffering, you will find grace in its many facets and colors."—Wm. Paul Young, *The Shack*

CHAPTER 6
OH, WHAT FUN IT IS TO RIDE!

"Laughter is an instant vacation." —Milton Berle

"My grandmother started walking five miles a day when she was sixty. She's ninety-seven now, and we don't know where she is." —Ellen DeGeneres

Where does a snowman keep his money?
In a snow bank.

What does a snowman eat for breakfast?
Frosted Flakes.

Speaking of flakes, did you hear the one about Adolf Hitler? (What a transition!) When he saw his chances of winning slipping away, he went to an astrologer. "Am I going to lose the war?" "Yes!" she says as she stares into her crystal ball. "Am I

*going to die soon?" "Yes!" came the reply, "on a Jewish holiday!"
"Which one?" he asks. "Any day you die will be a Jewish
holiday!"*—a joke from a concentration camp

*"... you have to laugh at the things that hurt you just to keep
yourself in balance, just to keep the world from running you
plumb crazy."*—Ken Kesey, *One Flew Over the Cuckoo's Nest*

Nothing made my dad more determined to do something
than telling him he couldn't, so when the doctors told him
he would never walk again, he was determined to prove them
wrong. Several times a day, my mom would half walk, half carry
him up and down the hallway. My mom showed incredible
strength, at least as much as my dad. Much of what I learned
about life and marriage, I learned from watching her care for
my dad. She married "for better or for worse," and for many
years, she got "the worse" in the "sickness and in health" deal.
She was a few months pregnant when my dad left for Korea. It
would be two years before she saw him again. He carried the
wounded to get help. Now, she was carrying him.

As my dad regained some strength, he got those big metal
crutches that wrap around your forearms so he could walk the
hall on his own. As it got warmer, he started up and down
our fifty-yard driveway to our house, which sat atop a hill. It
became part of his daily routine. Walk down, get the mail, and
walk back up. Strength was one thing, balance was another.

His inner ear was removed during the operation, adding to the challenge.

"Scott! Glenn!! Come quick!" My mom's voice sounded alarmed, but not panicked. My mom never panicked. It had been a hard, long year. Now, as snow lay on the ground, so did my dad. We had spent the morning shoveling snow. No small task. But why buy a snow blower, or pay a man with a plow on his truck, when you have four kids and four perfectly good shovels? Mom and dad would help, too—normally. You knew he wanted to help; would giving anything to help. Now, all he could do was stand at the window, the same window where he once watched us sled. Our front hill was the best spot for sledding, and the whole street would come when we had a storm. We kept our six-man toboggan in the garage next to the shovels and near the door so we could get to it quickly.

On this day, he would have happily stood at that window.

We pulled on our boots and grabbed the toboggan on the run

Happier times with my dad, in another uniform he loved.

as my mom used her voice to yell down that "Help is on the way!"

There were no major injuries to my dad's body, but the look of disappointment and failure on his face was palpable. We rolled his 6'1", 200-pound-plus frame onto the toboggan and pulled him up the drive. He didn't say a word. No one did. But it was clear he was crushed he couldn't even walk up the hill of the driveway anymore.

I have so many memories of sledding down that hill with my dad. My brothers and sister would get in a line, and my dad would start down the hill on his belly, and one by one, we piled on. The home movies of this are among my favorite. We would climb on the Flexible Flyer and he would pull on the rope, faster and faster, yanking it left and right, trying to get us to fall off.

But here we were pulling a grown man up a driveway. His driveway. It was a very sad moment. Panting and straining as we got near the top, I got this idea. Maybe it's time for a role reversal. And just before we got to the garage, I turned the sled around, away from the driveway, and ran as fast as I could down the front hill, pulling my dad on the sled.

Sometimes you don't know whether to laugh or cry, but if you get to choose, laugh. It's okay to cry, too, but in that moment, as the snow came down, my gift rose up. I got "gleeful."

I can't repeat everything he said. Something like "What in Sam Hill are you doing? Hey... hey!" But about halfway down the hill, as we approached Mach 3, I looked back and saw a smile. A snow-covered face with a smile. My job here was done. So, I left him and went inside to get my coat. NOOOO! We pulled him back up, and that was that. There were no "Thank yous," no pep talks, no discussion of the event. Thoughts and feelings were rarely discussed in our house. We just lived out my mom's philosophy of life: "You just do what you have to do!" And I did what I had to do; the only thing I could do, really. The only thing I seemed good at—trying to bring some joy to a miserable situation.

Something changed while going down that hill. One moment there was profound disappointment and disgust; the next, a moment of sheer delight! A Smile replaced Sadness, and it was worth it, even for a moment.

His legs did not get any better. In fact, they never would. He didn't give up, though. He made it another eight years before surrendering to the wheelchair permanently. He was able to walk my sister

> *"I have seen what a laugh can do. It can transform the almost unbearable into something bearable, even hopeful."* —Bob Hope

down the aisle on her wedding day, meeting an unspoken goal. That determination never left. There's a lot to be said for not giving up, no matter how long the odds. That's what made him my hero.

There is now scientific evidence that laughter really does help us heal and cope with the worst things life throws at us. Even in the concentration camps, the Jewish prisoners used comedy to diffuse situations, mock their enemies, and build hope. Comedy is powerful, so use it. What makes you laugh? What cartoons or TV shows? What kind of jokes make you laugh? I've heard that kids in kindergarten laugh over four hundred times a day, but the average adult less than ten. The average Baptist? Less than five! And research says that the average adult needs twenty good laughs a day, so what are you waiting for?

"The most wonderful feeling in the world is when tears turn to laughter because someone didn't want you to be sad, and said something funny to cheer you up. Suddenly, you are lifted from a dark place and you know that everything really will be OK."
—Susan Gale

CHAPTER 7
ANGELS IN THE
LOCKER ROOM

How do angels greet each other?
HALO!

"The reason angels can fly is they take themselves lightly."—G.K. Chesterton

"I was a terrible baseball player. The only thing I caught was athlete's foot!"—Beth Brubaker

"The fans in the stands chanted louder and louder. 'We want Gordon! We want Gordon!' Our team was getting creamed, the game was hopeless, and I saw the coach make his way toward me. My heart began to beat faster. He found me sitting at my normal spot on the bench. 'Hey, Gordon!' 'Yes, Coach!' I said, grabbing my helmet. 'Some folks in the stands want you. Go see what they want!'"—Tommy Moore

I sat on the bench in the gym while our class cleaned out their lockers. Another school year was almost over, and it was nothing like the closing scene in *Grease*. There was no Olivia Newton-John looking good and walking toward me. No music played, and no kids danced. Just the thoughts of disappointment and dejection that danced in my head. Sitting on the bench was very familiar to me—it was where I spent my time during most of the games.

At a recent high-school reunion, folks were surprised to hear me share some of my struggles. "You were always so funny! I had no idea you were hurting." And to be honest, those feelings came and went. But when they came—hopelessness, anger, and self-hate were overwhelming. In fact, most people at my reunion had similar stories, even the popular, good-looking ones.

In English class, I wrote a paper on why I hated life. I never attempted to take my life, but when my emotional rollercoaster would take a dip, the thought crossed my mind more than once. "If this is as good as life gets, then why bother?" was a recurring question. Maybe it's why I have such a heart for hurting kids today.

One teacher can make such a difference. Mine had a burr haircut and sharp Italian features. He wasn't tall or super muscular, but he had a presence. My gym teacher (and the football team's line coach), Mr. Morris DeFrank, was a man who demanded and got respect. Some teachers got respect through fear. Mr. DeFrank got it because he cared.

"Hey, Gordy, what's happening?" I loved that a coach knew my name when he talked to me. Coach DeFrank always asked how things were with my dad. My parents and the Gillespies started a parents sports booster club. In a small school in a small town, people know other people's business, but not many care. But when Coach D asked, he looked you in the eyes, his strong hands on your shoulders, and you could see that he truly felt bad that my dad was struggling. You knew from the look in his eyes and the tone of his voice that he cared for hurting kids. How many teachers can say the same?

As he headed toward his office, he said, "See ya at football camp, Gordy!"

"I don't think so, Coach!" I whispered.

"You're not going out for the team this year?" We were a new school, and though our girls teams had amazing winning records, our football team struggled against established teams. My alma mater, Garnet Valley, was actually in *Sports Illustrated* because the team with the longest losing streak in the nation… beat us! National news, and not what you need when you already have low self-esteem.

"I never get to play, Coach. Maybe I'll go out for cross country."

Somehow, the coaches hadn't seen the potential of a 5'11",

(L-R): Me, my brother Scott, and Coach DeFrank. The fact that Coach is still in my life after all these years shows you how important he was to me then and now.

125-pound football player. As most players do, I lied about my weight posted in the program. I exaggerated it to a whopping 133 pounds to strike fear in our opponents. But I never got off the bench, even when we were behind by thirty points. What was I going to do? Blow the game and ruin my coach's record? I hate that coaches don't give more kids a chance.

Somehow, holding dummies every practice so the superstars could run you over every day had lost its appeal. My dreams of being a star like my dad were fading. I just didn't seem to care about football, or anything else. That is a dangerous place to be at any age.

Coach DeFrank saw something and did something. He gave

me a job as his assistant trainer, taping ankles and helping in the training room. And I liked it. And with some encouragement, I did go out the next year. And with a rash of injuries that had nothing to do with my abilities as a trainer, we had a severe shortage of players. Well, what could they do? That's right— send in the benchwarmers. I got into a few junior varsity games, and my dad didn't believe it at first, so they made a bed for him in the back of our station wagon. My mom drove up on the field, a few feet from the end zone, and right next to the snack bar. They faced the back of the car toward

Me, warming up the bench.

the field so he could look out the tailgate window. After the game, he didn't mention the tackle I made at the five-yard line. Ever the coach, he pointed out a play where I was out of position and got beat. Compliments were rare, but I saw a bit of a smile, and would do almost anything to make him proud.

Years later, that field would be named Mo DeFrank Stadium. He not only taped ankles, he touched hearts and changed lives. He still sends me notes telling me he's proud of me. He marvels that I can use comedy to do some good in a world full of hurting folks. If you ever wonder where I got the idea, look in the mirror, Coach!

I WISH I KNEW

"One person can make a difference, and everyone should try."
—John F. Kennedy

I like to say it this way: "One person cannot change the world, but you can change the world for one person."

I wish I knew that there are seasons in life, and that seasons change. At a recent reunion, some were surprised to hear about my struggles with depression or what my dad went through. Some students I thought had it all together with good looks, good grades, and girlfriends and cool cars, confided in me that their home lives were a mess. They hid their pain and fear. Surrounded by multitudes, we somehow stay hidden in our own little worlds. It is not a safe place. We can get depressed if we are cut off from help, and think things will never change.

Not only can your life change, but you can help someone else change theirs, too. If we look around, there are a lot of Gordys sitting on those benches in every school or office. Sometimes all it takes is a kind word and a little interest to make a huge difference.

CHAPTER 8
THE BUTTERFLY EFFECT

What did one caterpillar say to the other caterpillar after seeing a butterfly? "You'll never get me up in one of those things!"

Dr. Emmett Brown: Then tell me, future boy, who is the president of the United States in 1985?
Marty McFly: Ronald Reagan.
Dr. Emmett Brown: Ronald Reagan? The actor? Who's the vice president? Jerry Lewis? And I suppose Jane Wyman is the first lady!
Marty McFly: Whoa. Wait, Doc!
Dr. Emmett Brown: And Jack Benny is secretary of the treasury!
—From *Back to the Future*

In Ray Bradbury's classic short story, *Sounds of Thunder*, we are taken 100 years to the future, to the year 2055. Time travel now exists, and hunters and NRA folks are still around. And for a fee, you can travel back in time to hunt dinosaurs. In order not to alter history, the hunters can only shoot dinosaurs close to death, and can never leave the special metal pathway hovering over the earth. But alas, for young Eckels, a creature comes toward him, and overcome by fear, he takes off, leaving the path. SPOILER ALERT. Eventually, he makes it back to the path and comes home. Upon his return, the world has changed. It is not as he remembers it. He gazes upon this new world, and as he looks down, he sees a butterfly trapped in the mud of his boot.

"The Butterfly Effect" became a real term that says, basically, that the flapping of the wings of a butterfly on one part of the world could start a tornado on the other side of the world. I am no scientist or mathematician, but I do know that something that happened 200 years ago profoundly affected my life.

In 1749, nearly thirty years before the Revolutionary War, a wedding took place. There was no scandal as a young Jacob Pyle pledged his eternal love to one Jane Sharpless. Details are sketchy, but safe to say there was no limo rides, or alcohol served, or wild dancing at The Friends meeting house in Concordville, Pennsylvania. Jacob and Jane were third generation worshippers in the Quaker tradition.

There are several stories of where the name "Quaker" originated. One tale says it was a derogatory term used by King Charles II to William Penn (the founder of Pennsylvania), who would not take his hat off in deference to his majesty.

Penn told the king that instead of worrying about silly things like hats, he should be "Quaking before the Lord." The king then responded, "Get this quaker out of here!" But rather than a band of rowdies starting a wild movement, a more quiet, contemplative style of worship and of life evolved as Quakers met in the Friends meeting houses. Even as a young movement, one concerned church leader said, "The Quakers have lost their quake."

Jacob and Jane had a son named John who fell in love with a girl named Alice Crosley from nearby Aston. It is just a few miles away as the crow flies, but worlds away from the Quaker tradition. To their parents' horror, they married "outside the faith," at St John's Episcopal on Cheyney Road in 1787. The Revolutionary War had just ended, and a nation was being born. Many people get confused here, with July 4th, 1776, firmly set in our minds. But that was when a group of Colonists declared independence. George Washington did not get sworn in as president until 1789. And it wasn't in Washington, DC, it was in New York City.

More than a country was born that year. A bouncing baby boy named Israel also came into the world. He must have found church boring, and longing for something more, Israel attended some of the early camp meetings. Folks from as far as twenty-five miles away, in Philadelphia, made the trip by horse and buggy to hear circuit riders like Francis Ashbury of the early Methodist movement.

Young Israel had a miraculous encounter with the living God. Historians say he was "dramatically converted." Oral history says he was so excited about his relationship with Jesus that he was "uninvited" from the more conservative church. He was charged with "excessive zeal." A Quaker with excessive zeal? I wonder what they looked like. How few in the church would be guilty of this today?

No longer welcome in the traditional church, he did something dramatic. In 1810, at the age of twenty-two, Israel helped build a place of worship. A little church named Stonybank Community Church. A few years later, and a few miles up the road, his brother-in-law, Albin Pyle, helped start the Bethlehem United Methodist church in 1842. And a few years after that, in the 1870's, Chester Heights Camp Meeting would be officially chartered. Trains and caravans of carriages came from Philadelphia and Wilmington, Delaware, to the outdoor chapel on the hill to meet with God.

If you looked at a map and drew a line from Stonybank to Chester Heights Camp meeting, then to Bethlehem Methodist Church, you get a triangle. And right dab inside that triangle would be the Douglas home. The Bermuda Triangle is known for mysterious disappearances and strange happenings. Well, within this ten-mile triangle outside Philadelphia, many supernatural things also took place. Sins vanished, the Spirit of God moved, and lives changed forever, mine included.

Two hundred years later, the breeze of the Spirit is still felt at

Stonybank Community Church, my home church when I was a kid. My family attended Sunday school, church picnics, and prayer meetings there. For over thirty years, I got to hear God's Word faithfully preached. On Sunday nights in the summer, we met at Chester Heights for great singing, fellowship, and old-time revival preaching. It was at Stonybank that I first served as the leader of the youth group, and later, the assistant pastor.

It was at Bethlehem Methodist where I met with Pastor Jon Svenson, who led a small group of pastors in monthly prayer meetings, something I still do with the new pastor, Tim Kriebel. It is where my grandsons now attend Awana. (Awana is kind of a Christian Boy Scouts.)

I WISH I KNEW

"I am looking forward to the future, and feeling grateful for the past!"—Mike Rowe, from *Dirty Jobs*

I wish I knew that I am what I am today, in part, because of a spiritual butterfly effect. Someone who lived 200 years ago did something that deeply affected my life today. Can you think of something in your town or state that is a part of your life today? And I wonder, should we last another 200 years, whose lives we might affect. But rather than wait, why not look for a way to touch someone's life today? Live your life with purpose. Start small, but be intentional. Your life can make a difference.

CHAPTER 9
WHAT GOES AROUND, COMES AROUND

"Money was very tight in my day. We bought generic everything, even butter. It was called 'I Can't Believe I Can't Afford I Can't Believe It's Not Butter! We couldn't afford hand sanitizer. We used something called Soapy Water. It killed 99.9% of dirt."— Clayburn Cox

*"When we were kids, if one of us kids in the neighborhood would have caught the Ebola virus, their mom would have spit in a Kleenex and wiped it off."—*Robert G. Lee

"Those Advil come with a candy coating. Did you notice that? And they are delicious, but they come with that warning: DO NOT TAKE MORE THEN TWO A DAY!! Hey, Advil, if you want us to only take two a day, leave off the candy coating!"— Mitch Hedberg

With my dad's family coming from Scotland, this story had special interest for me. It is about a poor Scottish farmer by the name of Fleming. One day, while working the fields trying to make a living for his family, he heard a cry for help coming from a nearby bog. That's a muddy swamp for ye city slickers. He dropped his tools and ran toward the cry.

There, mired waist deep in black muck, was a terrified boy, screaming and struggling to free himself. But the more he squirmed, the deeper he sank into the slop. Farmer Fleming saved the lad from what could have been a slow and terrifying death.

'Twas the very next day that a fancy carriage pulled up to the Scotsman's humble abode (in modern speak, "This rich dude in a sweet ride showed up to the tiny crib of the Scottish farmer). An elegantly dressed nobleman (the man was decked out) stepped out and introduced himself as the father of the boy Farmer Fleming saved.

"I want to repay you," said the nobleman. "You saved my son's life."

"No, I can't accept payment for what I did," the Scottish farmer replied, waving off the offer despite his many needs. At that moment, the farmer's own son came out of the door of their tiny home.

"Is that your son?" the nobleman asked.

"Yes," the farmer replied proudly.

"I'll make you a deal. Let me provide him with the level of education my own son will enjoy. If the lad is anything like his father, he'll no doubt grow to be a man we both will be proud of." And that he did.

Farmer Fleming's son attended the very best schools, and in time, graduated from St Mary's Hospital Medical School in London, where he went on to become known throughout the world as the noted Sir Alexander Fleming, the discoverer of penicillin.

Years afterward, the same nobleman's son was stricken with pneumonia. What saved his life this time? Penicillin.

And who was that nobleman with the fancy carriage? Lord Randolph Churchill. And his son's name? You know him as Sir Winston Churchill.

I WISH I KNEW

I wish I knew that not everything I do has an immediate effect. Someone once said, "What goes around, comes around." The Apostle Paul said it a bit differently: "You shall reap what you sow!" Sometimes you see results right away. Sometimes it may take years. Can you think of something you did in the past? Maybe something in your childhood that still has a good

> *"With every deed, you are sowing a seed, though the harvest you may not see."*—Ella Wheeler Wilcox

effect today, or something where you didn't see the results for years?

A little over a year ago, I stood in line at a funeral to offer comfort to a wonderful woman I work with, whose husband died suddenly. A middle-aged woman approached me. Funeral etiquette is almost nonexistent anymore. "Do you remember me?" I get asked that a lot, and most times, like this time, I have no clue who these people are. I meet about 1000 people a week—that adds up quickly. I tried to cut the conversation short, as this was no place for a celebrity sighting. "You did a fundraiser to help my husband and I adopt a little boy from China thirteen years ago. We are so grateful our lives are changed. I thought you might want to see him. He's right over there!"

Across the foyer, a group of teens had gathered. I'm no Sherlock Holmes, but despite the modern American wardrobe, I could pick out the kid from China. There he was, happy, healthy, and hanging with some friends. It is hard to describe the conflicting emotions I felt being with a friend in the midst of her grief, while sharing the joy of a mom looking at a son she almost didn't have. My little gift changed the life of someone on the other side of the globe. Deep down, part of me felt really good.

Sometimes figuring out what something is can be as difficult as seeing through an optical illusion. Can you spot the young woman and the old lady in William Ely Hill's famous My Wife and My Mother-in-Law sketch?

CHAPTER 10
WHERE THERE'S A
"WILL," THERE'S A WAY

"Little Alex is mean. One day, Alex gets bitten by a dog with rabies. The doctor gives him some painful shots and tells him to lie still to see if there is a reaction. A few minutes later, the doctor comes back in the room and sees little Alex writing furiously. 'There is no need to panic!' said the doctor. 'You don't need to write out a will!' 'This isn't my will,' says Alex. 'This is a list of people I want to bite!'"—Milton Berle

Why don't oysters give to charity?
Because they're Shellfish!—Jay Leno

The Army used to have a commercial to help recruit high-school students. Four guys about to graduate high school sat in a booth at a fast-food joint. They ask each other, "What are you going to do?" "I don't know. What are you going to do?" Three of them are clueless, but one says, "I'm going to see the world! Do you want that pickle?"

It was a similar scene for me just weeks before graduation. I was sitting with some friends at the same table in the cafeteria we'd sat at for four years. Pretty far away from the cool kids, even farther from the one with all the pretty girls. It was pretty close to where the vo-tech kids sat. We didn't know them well—they only went to school with us half a day, then went off somewhere to learn a trade. Many of us "college prep" students looked down on those poor students who didn't quite have the smarts we did. We were wrong! At our reunion, many of those guys and gals have their own businesses and did quite well.

With graduation around the corner, the discussion at our table centered on that same question: "What are you going to do?" And most of us had the same answer, "I don't know!" But my friend, Craig Baillie, said he wanted to go to Williamson trade school. I had never heard of it, but my dad was big on learning a trade, so, I checked it out. It was just a few miles from our home, and it was free. Yes, a college that was free. With my dad out of work, and money tighter than ever, that sounded good. Weeks before graduating, because of a comment in a cafeteria, I applied to what is now called the Williamson College of the Trades. I was accepted, and the next three years changed my life in ways I could have never imagined.

Here is an excerpt from an article on Isaiah Williamson's

amazing life taken from *Philanthropy Roundtable* by Christopher Levenick, with some personal comments added.

Isaiah Williamson was born on February 4, 1803, near Bensalem Township in Bucks County, Pennsylvania. The son of devout Quakers, he was one of eight children, a farm boy who learned early on the value of industry, frugality, and honesty. At the age of fifteen, he apprenticed himself to Harvey Gillingham, who ran a nearby country store. Within seven years, Williamson saved $2,000. It was enough money to move to Philadelphia and open his own dry goods business, which grew rapidly. By 1838, at thirty-five years of age, with assets worth approximately $100,000 (roughly $2 million today), he retired, spending the next few years touring Europe.

Can you imagine retiring at thirty-eight, or taking a few years off? What was it like to travel the world before cars and airplanes? Apparently, Williamson was unsuited for the life of a dilettante. He returned to Philadelphia, where he invested his money in real estate and promising enterprises like railroads. By the 1880s, he was known to be one of the wealthiest men in the commonwealth, with an estimated fortune of $20 million (approximately $500 million today). He was equally famous for his thrift, allegedly eating only some bread crust for a meal and making one suit last as long as most men had two.

As he entered the last decades of his life, philanthropy

My roommate Craig and I during the holidays. I believe you know the man in the middle.

engaged more and more of Williamson's attention. He is believed to have given away millions of dollars during his lifetime. Determining the extent of his generosity has always been difficult; virtually all of his donations were made under strict conditions of secrecy or under the pseudonym "Hez." His generosity helped build and support scores of asylums and orphanages, hospitals and benevolent societies, libraries, seminaries, colleges, and universities.

John Wanamaker, a close friend and fellow philanthropist

and entrepreneur, is best known as the founder of Wanamaker's department store. Wanamaker wrote in the only book-length biography of Williamson: "He was invariably strongly moved to help the man who was trying to help himself, however humble the effort. But for mere beggars, low or high, he had little sympathy."

As early as the 1850's, as Isaiah walked the streets of Philadelphia, he saw a scene not too different from the one Will Smith paints in the theme song to *The Prince of Bel-Air*. Sing it with me now:

"In west Philadelphia born and raised,
On the playground was where I spent most of my days...."

Yes, Mr. Williamson saw kids getting attacked by guys who were "up to no good." But unlike Will Smith's character, their parents lacked the resources to do something about it. They didn't have rich relatives in Bel-Air, or even the Main Line, so he took it upon himself to help. As Mr. Williamson told Wanamaker, "It was seeing boys, ragged and barefooted, playing or lounging about the streets, growing up with no education, no trade, no idea of usefulness, that caused me to think of founding a school where every boy could be taught some trade, free of expense."

Williamson College archivist Leslie Carey explained the situation to me, as I always thought it was the boys orphaned during the Civil War who stirred Isaiah's heart. "[You must] understand that poverty was not new after the Civil War. The 1800's had a high incidence of both infant and maternal mortality (translate that to a lot of babies and mothers died in childbirth). Great numbers of contagious diseases like tuberculosis, diphtheria, and small pox also took many lives. Then there were farming and industrial accidents due to unregulated and un-inspected machinery and a lack of any social safety net like family aid, foster care, or Social Security. There were no drug stores on every corner, or clinics for miles. All of these factors contributed to a high number of orphaned boys (and girls) in Mr. Williamson's lifetime." All this multiplied greatly the number of fatherless families.

On December 1, 1888, Mr. Williamson executed his plan. "He had to be wheeled from his carriage in a rolling chair," wrote Wanamaker, "but his spirit was alert and joyful."

Williamson committed $2.1 million (roughly $50 million in present value) to the project. Unfortunately, Williamson soon fell ill, dying less than two weeks later. Yet, his plans were well laid. The school was built on a beautiful site of 211 acres outside Media, Pennsylvania. "In this country," Williamson explained, "every able-bodied, healthy young man who has learned a good mechanical trade, and is truthful, honest, frugal, temperate, and industrious, is certain to succeed in life, and to become a useful and respected member of society."

In his will, Mr. Williamson clearly stipulated that in considering admissions to the school, "preference shall always be given to the poor." And it is true to this day. The school recruits young men from the region's toughest areas, working closely with ministers, guidance counselors, coaches, and other mentors to find promising young men who would benefit from learning a trade. The school still provides a full scholarship for all its students, not one penny of which comes from public sources.

So, what courses of study are offered at Williamson College of the Trades? There are shops that teach carpentry, masonry, landscaping, machine tools, painting, and power-plant for all its students, not one penny of which comes from public sources. Mike Rowe, host of *Dirty Jobs* and *Somebody's Gotta Do It*, said "We are churning out a generation of poorly educated people who have no skills, no ambition, no guidance, and no realistic expectation of what it means to work!"

All students are required to live on campus in supervised dormitories, attend a daily chapel service, and conform to the dress code. Besides the book learning, there is hands-on learning and an emphasis on core values of Faith, Excellence, Diligence, Integrity, and Service.

Mr. Williamson never saw me, but he saw boys like me. Instead of complaining or condemning, he contributed. And my life and thousands of others were changed, and the world is a better place.

I WISH I KNEW

"I view myself as slightly above average in talent. What I do have is a ridiculous, sickening work ethic; an obsession to practice and preparation. Fame and success doesn't change you, it only amplifies what is inside. I want the world to be better because I was here!"—Will Smith

What's in your wallet? Or, better yet, what is in your will? Ever think that far ahead? Most don't. Jack Benny left money and instructions to deliver a long-stemmed rose to his wife, Mary, every day after his death. Billionaire Leona Helmsley left $12 million dollars to her nine-year-old dog named Trouble. Portuguese aristocrat Luis Carlos de Noronha Cabral da Camera left a considerable fortune to seventy people picked randomly from a phone book. Fred Baur, inventor of Pringles potato chips, had his ashes sealed in a Pringles can when he died. Even more bizarre was Mark Gruenwald, writer of *Captain America*. He gave instructions to have his ashes mixed with ink and put in a special edition of another comic book, Squadron Supreme. Comedian David Brenner asked that $100 in small bills be stuffed in his sock, "Just in case there is tipping where I am going." What a combination of sentimental, strange, and just plain silly requests.

I wish I knew that I could be part of the solution. Whether it is in the workplace or in the world, we see problems. And the problems appear so big that we often think there is nothing we can do, but assessing the problems and my resources, what I can do is start. Start by touching one life, solving one problem. Start by asking yourself, "Who can I help?"

CHAPTER 11
HERE COMES DA JUDGE!

"Just because you did it, doesn't mean you are guilty!"—A Billboard for Lawyer Larry Archie

"Look at the judge. A guy who spends half his life in school. He is a lawyer, then he is a lower judge, then an upper judge. He works his way up to some big important murder trial like this, and he doesn't even get to decide if the guy is guilty or not. No, that decision is made by five salesmen, three plumbers, two bank tellers, and a dingbat."—Archie Bunker in *All in the Family*

Famed comedian W.C. Fields lay quite ill in the hospital. A friend came to visit, and as he entered the room, he was shocked to see W.C. with a Bible in his hands staring intently and flipping through page after page. "What are you doing? I've never known you to be a religious man." To which W.C. replied in his wonderful way, "LOOPHOLES! I'm looking for LOOPHOLES!"

R*owan & Martin's Laugh-In* was a TV sensation, made for people like me with ADD. Have I mentioned that I have ADD? Laugh-In was an hour-long program of nonstop silliness. A rapid-fire combination of gags, one-liners, and sketches, it made stars of folks like Ruth Buzzi as Gladys Ormphby, with her drab sweater, hairnet, and lethal purse. Goldie Hawn dancing in a bikini while telling classic dumb blonde jokes. Can you see Arte Johnson as the German soldier peeking through the bushes saying, "Verrrry interesting..."? And the phrase "Here comes da judge! Here comes da judge!" was made popular when Sammy Davis, Jr. re-created an old burlesque routine by veteran vaudeville star Pigmeat Markham.

A little TV history. When George Schlatter asked Sammy Davis to do this routine, he agreed, but only on the condition that Pigmeat appear on the next episode. This not only rejuvenated Markham's career, but gave him a whole new audience, for until that time he had only appeared to white audiences. My how times have changed, in part because of what Sammy Davis, Jr. did.

Some people say Pigmeat "invented" rap, but in those days it was called syncopated patter. So, the scene started with a rap beat to Pigmeat saying, "Hear ye, hear ye/the court of Swing/is just about ready to do that thing./I don't want no tears, I don't want no lies/Brother, I don't want no alibis!"

The sketch mocked the typical courtroom etiquette and made hilarious rulings on cases. Today, there are a ton of judges on TV: Judge Judy, Mills Lane, Judge Mathis, and Joe Brown. Growing up, we had shows with courtrooms, like *Perry Mason*, but our only TV show with a real judge was *The People's Court* with Judge Wapner. Over 2,300 verdicts were rendered over twelve years. It touches something in our minds. We love the drama, and we want a verdict. Even *The Reader's Digest* has a regular feature called "You Be the Judge" where the facts of a case are presented, and you get to guess how the court ruled.

Most of us don't do that with questions about God. How do we come to conclusions about the existence of God and other eternal issues? Do you believe the *Bible* is true? Why or why not? Did Jesus really live? Did He do miracles? And what about that whole death on the Cross and coming back to life thing? Could that have really happened?

Like many college-age kids, I was cocky and thought I had everything figured out, even though my life was a mess. While at Williamson College of the Trades, a young man named Steve handed me a tract and asked if I knew I was going to heaven. It was a little blue leaflet. It had multiple choices. But on something like this, do you really want to guess? On the cover was the question "Are you going to heaven?" Inside were these choices:

"I am going to heaven because:

- I go to church
- I keep the Ten Commandments
- I never killed anybody
- I give money to the poor
- I am basically a good person (at least compared to some people I know)"

Not wanting anything to do with God, church, or religion, I tried to blow him off. "God, Buddha, Confucius, it doesn't matter—they all same the same thing."

"Have you ever read what Buddha or Confucius say about sin, heaven, or hell?"

"Well, no, but…"

He continued. "Have you compared it to what the *Bible* says?"

Ah, I got him now. "You can't trust the *Bible*. It has been translated so many times, and there are so many versions, you don't know which one to believe. And," I said, now on a roll as other students in the dorm listened in, "the *Bible* is filled many contradictions!" Game, set, and match—I win!! My two biggest arguments in less than a minute. Now, let me get on with the rest of my life and not worry about eternity.

But Steve didn't leave. He handed me his *Bible* and asked me to show him one. One what? "Show me a contradiction." WAIT. TIME OUT. TIME OUT. FOUL!!!

I had nothing to back up my views, just pat clichés on faith, but I had never really researched it. How could I make a judgment on something so important so flippantly? Steve was part of a group of college kids that met at a house near Grace Chapel in Havertown, Pennsylvania. He invited some of us to come out and join them. *Oh, this will be great,* I thought. *A bunch of drugged-up hippies sitting in the living room singing Kumbaya.*

But I went. Not because of any interest in spiritual things, but because Steve said there were girls from area nursing schools there. When you are at an all-boys school, any mention of females grabs your attention. God sure knows how to bait a hook.

One night, our group went to Manoa Presbyterian Church to hear some guy named Josh McDowell. Josh had a very, very rough childhood, and was in pre-law when some students confronted him about Jesus. Determined to shut them all up, and to be fair, he would use only "evidence" that could be submitted in a court of law. After hundreds of hours of research in the world's best libraries, Josh was overwhelmed. He wrote a book called *Evidence That Demands a Verdict*. It has now sold millions and millions of copies around the world.

I can still hear him (because I bought the cassette tape). "Tonight, I want you to use your minds. I don't want you to shelve your brains, I want you to use them. I know there are some here tonight who are skeptical. Some are seekers, and some just want to argue. But all I am asking you is to weigh the evidence and evaluate it." And then he presented it with humor, with passion, and he talked fast. I liked that! It was one of the best speeches, or sermons, I have ever heard.

Now what do I do? This guy had tough things in his childhood like me. He asked the same questions as me. But he researched this more than me. Was the *Bible* really true? Was Jesus really who He claimed to be? I grew up hearing, and even reciting, every communion Sunday that "Jesus Christ was crucified, died, and was buried, and on the third day, ascended into heaven and sitteth at the right hand of God." But what did that mean?

I had to become a judge. Did you know that there are thousands of manuscripts of the *Bible*, in different languages, dating back to within one hundred years of Christ's life? They can be compared and contrasted to see if anything changed. Yes, the *Bible* has many different versions and translations because it spread through the world. And language, even for us Americans, has changed. Didn't George Carlin have a routine highlighting this? "What's hot?" was replaced with "Cool." "What's up?" became "What's going down?" People of different ages use different words and phrases; people in different parts of the country have distinctive speech and colloquial terms. It doesn't take much study of the *Bible* to see what has and hasn't changed. Compared to any other work of literature, the *Bible's* message remains unchanged. A message of love, forgiveness, and hope centered around a person named Jesus. Could it be true?

"After 500 hours of research and study in the world's leading libraries," Josh concluded, "I have come to the conclusion that the resurrection of Christ is one of the most vicious, heartless hoaxes ever foisted on mankind, or it is the most fantastic fact in history. The greatest farce, or the greatest fact."

My life was about to change, although I didn't change my mind because of what Josh said. At least not yet. I had some thinking to do. I postponed my verdict on the *Bible*, not yet ready to put my faith in this Jesus Messiah guy.

But how about you? What do you believe about the *Bible*? Is it true? Is it trustworthy? Does it have errors and contradictions? Does it say the same things as other religions, or does it have a unique message? Most of the people I ask are like me at nineteen—they give flippant, pat answers, but have never investigated this for themselves.

My search and struggles continued a little longer, but eventually, like Josh, I was convinced.

And so, to quote Edith Ann, the Lily Tomlin character on *Laugh-In*, as she sat in her giant rocking chair, "AND THAT'S THE TRUTH!" And then she would stick out her tongue and give a big raspberry (how do you spell that?). "PFFFFFT!"

I WISH I KNEW

"It will greatly help you to understand Scripture if you note not only what is spoken and written, but of whom and to whom, with what words, at what time, where, to what intent, with what circumstances, considering what goes before and what follows."
—Miles Coverdale

Most of the problems people have with the *Bible* would disappear if they followed Miles Coverdale's advice. I wish I knew that some of the greatest minds over the last 2,000 years agree that the *Bible* is trustworthy, reliable, and life-changing, but people like Josh McDowell offer real research on this. *The Case for Christ* was written by investigative reporter Lee Stroebel, an atheist trying to prove the *Bible*, and his wife, wrong. If you want to do some deeper research, check out the

> *"Christianity has not been tried and found wanting; it has been found difficult and not tried."*
> —G.K. Chesterton

websites of Ravi Zacharias or Mike Licona. These two brilliant scholars travel the world and debate doubters on a university level. There are no new objections, and there are good answers to the questions skeptics have brought up for centuries. Are you willing to search for the truth? Are you willing to learn?

A FUN READ-ALOUD

Since *Laugh-In* often ended with the Fickle Finger of Fate, let's have some fun reading "Prodigal in F" out loud, courtesy of the original Redneck comedian, Justin Fennell.

Feeling footloose and frisky, a feathered-brained fellow forced his fond father to fork over his farthings. He flew far to foreign fields and frittered his fortune feasting fabulously with faithless friends. Finally, facing famine, fleeced by his fellows in folly, he found himself a feed flinger in a filthy farmyard! Fairly famishing, he feigned he would fill his frame with foraged food from the fodder fragments. "Fooey! My father's flunkies fare far fancier!" The frazzled fugitive fumed furvishly, frankly facing facts. Frustrated by failure and filled with foreboding, he fled forthwith to his family, and falling at his father's feet, he floundered forelonely, "Father, I have flunked and foolishly forfeited family favor." But the faithful father, forestalling further flinching, frantically flagged the flunkies to fetch forth the finest fatling and fix a feast! Well, the fugitive's fault-finding frater frowned on the fickle forgiveness of the former folderol. His fury flashed! But fussing was futile. For the far-sighted father figured "Such filial fidelity is fine!" What forbids fervent festivity? For the fugitive is found! Unfurl the flags with flaring. Let fun and frolic freely flow. For former failures are forgotten, and forgiveness forms the foundation for future fortune!

(And I'm not being facetious!)

73

CHAPTER 12
ARE THERE HAIRCUTS
IN HEAVEN?

"My wife's favorite singer is Billy Ray Cyrus. How is that possible in a free country? He wore a mullet. Remember that? A Mississippi Mudflap, a West Virginia Waterfall, a Tennessee top hat—it is all business in the front, and a party in the back. That is an achy breaky bad mistaky."—Rik Roberts

"Dad, can I borrow the car?" came the request from the teenage boy with long hair and torn jeans. "You know the deal, son. If you want to use the car, you need to get a haircut." Trying to appeal to his dad's religious side, the young lad appealed. "But Dad, Jesus had long hair, and I just want to be like Him." "That's great, son. It is true that Jesus had long hair, but remember, Jesus also walked everywhere he went!"—From the Files of Tommy Moore

"Hey, Fidel Castro, is that your beard, or are you sticking your head under your armpit again?"—Don Rickles

It was February, 1964, and the world was about to change. Pan Am Flight 101 left Heathrow Airport in London, headed for New York City. On board were four mop-headed boys who called themselves The Beatles. They had a few records that did well over here in the United States, and they were coming for an appearance on *The Ed Sullivan Show*. Their arrival not only kicked off a new era in music, but also in hairstyles. And they got me in some serious trouble.

My dad was old-school. Started each day with a can of Barbasol and a double-sided razor. This was followed by a splash of Aqua Velva, and a touch of Brylcreem to hold his pompadour perfectly in place. "A little dab will do ya!" and his morning routine would end with a little kiss from my mom as he headed out the door for work. A big change in his routine took place one Christmas, as he switched from Aqua Velva to a splash of Old Spice, a gift from us kids.

Appearance is very important to teens, and I had several things going against me. First was a case of acne that single-handedly kept Clearasil in business for ten years. One of my early jokes was "I start every day doing the 3 S's… Seek, Squeeze, and Splatter! My mirror looked like a relief map of the Himalayas." Gross, huh?

Besides The Beatles, heartthrobs had long, wavy hair, including Bobby Sherman and David Cassidy. Even the clean-cut Tom Netherton, the tall, good-looking blonde from *The Lawrence Welk Show*, had perfect (though long) hair. Singer Tony Orlando, or Vinnie Barbarino on *Welcome Back, Kotter* had hairstyles that looked like my mom's yearbook picture. Wonder what happened to that actor who played Vinnie.

But concerning hairstyles, I had many inspirations. Tragically, my mom cut my hair. She did this for all, or to all, of us boys. Anything to save a buck.

Two words you never want to hear during a haircut are "Whoops!" and "Sorry." She meant well and did her best. Sometimes she would lie and say, "You look fine!" Other times, "It will grow back." Sometimes, I just wanted my ear to stop bleeding. She went for speed, not accuracy.

I wanted long hair. Not long like the rock bands, but long enough to cover my ears. I needed that. God has a sense of humor and allowed me to have full-sized ears at birth. Ears I could grow into. As a kid, I looked like a taxi with the doors open. I could get satellite TV before HBO was invented. In my mind, if I could get a cool car and get my hair to cover my ears—and do that perfect wave across my forehead, girls would come running.

But to my dad, long hair was a slap in the face of all America stood for, and no boys of his were going to look like hippies. One day, at nineteen, I put my foot down. I refused to get my hair cut. Words were said, lines were drawn, and I was asked to leave. Well, looking back, I wasn't asked. It was a command.

Loud and clear. "Leave now and do not come back home without a haircut and a new attitude." Looking back, it was so stupid. Years of tension followed that ultimatum between my dad and me.

I left home and went back to Williamson. As I walked down the hall, I noticed the class pictures of every class since 1888. Observation Number One: people rarely smiled in photographs until after 1950. Times were tough. Most of these boys were struggling and were separated from whatever family they had. There were no telephones to call home; no cars to come pick you up. Homesick in a tough world made for some somber looks. And with my heavy heart, and hair touching my ears, I would fit in pretty good in class of 1931.

Observation Number Two: hairstyles seem to change about every ten years. There seems to be a clear pattern for over 100 years. I know how girls' hairstyles change. My sister with the long hair parted down the middle in the early '70s. Then there was the Dorothy Hamill look, short and cute. The hit television show, *Charlie's Angels*, gave women three hairstyle choices, but the Farrah Fawcett feathered-look dominated, until the high hair of the 1980's exploded. All that hairspray might have something to do with global warming!

So, it was Christmas time, and to avoid a family feud, I spent more than a few weekends with my roommate, Craig, up in Schuylkill Haven, PA. Oh, and that Bible study from Grace Chapel, they were going on a "retreat." I wasn't sure what a "retreat" was, but I went for two good reasons. It wasn't home, and girls would be there.

There were fun games called "icebreakers." The boys and girls got to do cool stuff, like putting a toothpick between your teeth and passing a lifesaver between boys and girls. It was almost like kissing, without the saliva. Mostly, we were taught stuff about the *Bible*, or from the *Bible*. This went on for several hours a day, but the speaker was interesting. Rick Rodriquez was a Marine from Vietnam. Not a tall guy, not a loud guy, but one you clearly didn't want to mess with.

On Saturday night, the service took a dramatic turn. He said we had some decisions to make. He reminded us that the *Bible* was true, and that the *Bible* said we all had the problem of sin. I am not sure who gave him a list about me, but he mentioned how people like me were angry, had filthy mouths, and bad attitudes. Like he had watched a video of my life. He mentioned stealing, and lust, and lying. Each time he mentioned a sin, I knew he was talking about me. I felt convicted; I felt horrible. Rick said, "The wages of sin are death." Because of what I had done, what each of us has done, we deserve to be separated from God forever. I can't remember feeling so sorry for anything in my life.

With the command of a drill sergeant, Rick said, "I don't know why God loves you, but He does. ("Ya bunch of dirty, rotten sinners" is what I inferred.) He sent His Son, Jesus, to die on a cross to pay the debt you deserve. "You all know John

3:16, don't ya?" I memorized it this way: "For God so loved the world that He sent His only begotten Son, that whosoever believeth in Him, should not perish but have everlasting life."

Rick then said, "Put your name in that verse and say it again."

"For God so loved Gordon that He sent His Son for Gordon, and if Gordon would believe in HIM, Gordon would have everlasting life." Pastor Rick continued. "When Jesus was on the Cross, He was dying in your place." I knew Jesus died on the Cross. I had heard that my whole life, but I didn't know He did it for me. In fact, Rick said, "If you were the only person on earth, Jesus would have still come and died for you. He loves you that much. He wants you in His family. He wants to spend eternity with you." Whoa, this was blowing me away.

No wonder they call it *Amazing Grace*. No matter what you've done, where you've been, or how far you've fallen, you can start a new life today. Could there be any better news than this? You don't have to go to church, read your *Bible*, or give money to the poor. Those are all good things, but they won't cover your sin. Quoting from Ephesians 2:8-9: "For it is by grace you have been saved, through faith—and this is not from yourselves, it is the gift of God, not by works, so that no man can boast."

No man is good enough to qualify for heaven. God demands perfection. No man is able to do enough to qualify him for heaven. The debt was paid, the gift is offered.

Our part—my part—was to recognize my sin. And trust,

or believe that when Jesus died on the Cross, it was enough to make me acceptable in God's sight. Rick said, "The wages of sin are death, but the gift of God is eternal life." It is a gift. You must believe it to receive it. Then Rick said something I've never heard in a church service before. I asked him recently if my memory was accurate, and he said, in this case, yes.

Rick said loud and clear, "Nobody bow your head, nobody close your eyes. LOOK AT ME! GOD LOVES YOU and wants you in His family! He is willing to forgive you for every sin you ever committed. You confess your sin to Him, and He gives you His righteousness, a new life, a new start! It is a gift." He got louder as he went on. "Now, LOOK AT ME. I don't want you to slip up your hand with no one watching. I am tired of wimpy Christians when we need warriors. No more sissies; we need soldiers. If you won't stand up for Jesus in front of your friends, you won't stand up for Jesus in front of your schools. So, if you want this gift of forgiveness and new life, I want you to stand up right now and pray with me. Who will be first?"

I am not sure of all the theology, but I was sure I was a sinner. I think I always knew that—I just didn't know I could be forgiven. I wanted a new life. I wanted to know this kind of love. I wanted to be part of a family that loved like this. I was so truly sorry for the things I said and did that tears ran down my cheeks. I was willing to change, which I learned has something to do with repentance. My dad had said, "Do not come back here without a new haircut and a new attitude."

Jesus said, "Come as you are. I can take care of the hair—and the attitude—later."

The next thing I heard was "Thank you, Gordon. We have one!" I really don't remember standing, or even thinking of standing, but there I was, standing in the front row of seats in a cabin in the Pocono Mountains. A minute or so later, I prayed a simple prayer along with Rick and about a dozen others.

"Dear Jesus, I know I have sinned. I am sorry for the things I've said and done and thought. I believe you died on the Cross for me, and that, somehow, my sins were paid for. Please forgive me for all I have done. I want You to come into my life and be my Savior and Lord."

There were no fireworks. I was aware that I was blowing snot bubbles in front of the girls I wanted to impress. What a thing to notice. But there was more. There was peace and joy in my heart.

What happened in the next hour or so was amazing, and maybe more details will come in Volume Two of *Things I Wish I Knew*. What I remember is a girl saying, "Gordon, welcome to the family!" and hugging me. In fact, there was a whole group of girls waiting to hug me. Did I just die and go to heaven?

At the end of the cassette by Josh McDowell, he said something like this: "If you prayed that prayer tonight and you really meant it, I want you to go home and start reading the *Bible*. I suggest the Book of John. Read it every day for a

> "What exactly did Jesus accomplish by dying?" She was looking out into the forest.
>
> "Nothing much. Just the substance of everything that love purposed before the foundations of Creation," Papa stated matter-of-factly.
>
> "Honey, you asked me what Jesus accomplished on the cross, so now listen to me carefully: through His death and resurrection, I am now fully reconciled to the world."
>
> "The whole world? You mean those who believe in You, right?" The whole world, Mack, All I am telling you is that reconciliation is a two-way street, and I have done my part, totally, completely, finally. It is not the nature of love to force a relationship, but it is the nature of love to open the way."
>
> —Wm. Paul Young, *The Shack*

month, and if you are sincere, you will see dramatic changes in your actions and attitudes." Good advice. I don't care what label you put on the outside, or what denomination you go by, I only care if Jesus is on the inside. And if He is, it should change how you talk, and live, and treat people. A line or two from my favorite hymn:

What a wonderful change in my life has been wrought, since Jesus came into my heart. Floods of joy o'er my soul, like the sea billows roll, since Jesus came into my heart.
—Charles H. Gabriel and Rufus McDaniel

Now, what about how we look? I am still not sure if there are haircuts in heaven, but I know this: after the retreat—I went home with a new haircut and a new attitude. And my language changed a lot. I was shocked at how foul my tongue had become. If what comes out of the mouth is a sign of what is in your heart, I was in big trouble. Not everything changed that day, but it was the start of a new life.

The rest of this book will address some of the biggest blessings and battles I would face, and lots more funny stuff. Some amazing doors were about to open for me, and all because I had a joy and a peace to go with my new haircut and new attitude. What could go wrong? I should know by now— never ask what can go wrong.

Gordon Douglas

A classic *Can You Spot the Difference?* puzzle by
Earl Musick.

Life is a lot like one of these drawings. Everyone is different. Some differences you can spot right away, others are more subtle. This would be true of my life. Some big changes and some small. And some that happened quickly, while others took much longer. We are all at different places on our journey, but if this Christianity thing is real, you should be able to "spot the differences."

CHAPTER 13
UNLIKELY HEROES

"Ever find yourself in a situation when you wish you were MacGyver? When you could fix any problem with a paperclip, chewing gum, and pantyhose? My problem would be, 'Where in the world am I going to get... a paperclip?'"—Mike Williams

"I have a really bad mechanic. He couldn't fix my brakes, so he made the horn louder!"—Tommy Moore

"Murphy's Law for Mechanics—that moment you are under the car, with your hands over your head, covered in grease, your nose will itch, and you will have a sudden urge to tinkle."—Gordon Douglas, adapted from a classic joke.

I am a fixer. It is an addiction. I can't help myself. From leaky faucets to wobbly chairs, I like fixing things. And I'm pretty good at it. But when I became a pastor, it got a whole lot harder. Broken hearts, broken marriages, broken people filled my world, and I didn't know what to do. Bible school was great at teaching me how we got the *Bible*, and why we trust the *Bible*. We learned a lot of things we should do, and even more things we shouldn't! But all this information didn't always translate into increased love for God or practical help for the hurting folks in my life.

To paraphrase a rather crude bumper sticker, "Stuff Happens!" Bad stuff; hurtful stuff. One of the best courses I had in seminary was an introduction to counseling. We had a guest speaker who drew a picture of a big frame on the blackboard. Kids, this is before white boards with markers that smell bad, and can get you high. The only white was the chalk dust that got on your hands and pants. As he drew a big box, a frame of sorts, he said every person has a theology. Most of us believe if we just do certain things, God will reward us with certain things. We have a silent agreement with God. If we read our *Bible*, go to church, don't murder anyone, and give some money to charity, God will give us a nice house, a good-looking spouse, and a problem-free life. Sound familiar? Your deal might be slightly different, but I'm guessing it's close. God and me, we got a deal. If I do the right stuff, my life—my box—will be filled with nice things, and all the bad things stay outside the box.

But life isn't like that. Bad things happen. Cars crash, cancer kills, and parents part. Horrible, painful things that were outside our frame are now in our lives. When that happens—and it will—people have two choices: throw away the frame and turn from God because He didn't do what you expected, or get a bigger frame that explains why horrible things exist in this world. I wanted answers, and as I sought them, they came from a place and a person I would have never guessed. An artist answered and profoundly touched my life.

In 1976, a copy of a book named *Joni* was given to me. I never heard of Joni (pronounced like the boy's name Johnny), and I'm guessing there are many of you who haven't heard her story either. Joni was sixteen, active in sports, and loved the outdoors and horses. But when she dove into the shallow waters of the Chesapeake Bay, her life would never be the same. She fractured several vertebrae in her neck, leaving her paralyzed from the shoulders down. She spent months strapped to a bed. She no longer rides horses, but rather a motorized wheelchair.

Her first book grabbed my attention and stirred my heart. Joni is brutally honest about her struggles with anger, disappointment, and depression. No simple answers, no pie-in-the-sky theology. Not only did I struggle with these issues as a "normal walking person," but my dad was living this out before me! It was the right book at the right time.

She, like so many others, longed to be "made well" and sought healing. There are at least fifteen books on my shelves on the subject of healing. I long to see more people experience breakthroughs and miracles in their lives. Joni has now written fifty books. Two of my favorites address the toughest questions in life. *When God Weeps* and *Glorious Intruder* tackle (with tenderness and truth) the whole issue of where is God when I am suffering. Why did this happen? Or maybe you are asking, "Why is this happening?"

It has been a long, hard road for Joni. Like my dad, she can no longer walk or dress herself. She needs someone to turn her over in bed every couple of hours to prevent bed sores. But let me tell you what she can do. She can talk, and she can teach. When I first heard her speak, it had been almost a decade after her tragic accident, and Joni was gaining national attention for her artwork. Artwork? Yes, she paints incredibly detailed and beautiful pictures by holding paintbrushes in her mouth. Our family has gotten calendars and Christmas cards featuring her incredible artwork (note the pictures below).

Joni also sings. She has a beautiful voice that goes with her

A sampling of Joni Eareckson Tada's amazing artwork.

beautiful smile, and I've listened to her albums over and over again. She made a *Hymns for a Kid's Heart* CD that is awesome.

The first time we met was at a pastors event in Philadelphia. Joni, along with a pastor named Steve Estes, teamed up for a fantastic conference. She did a practical drama on how to speak to someone in a wheelchair. She and her assistant acted out some hilarious examples, and some not-so-funny things, people have said and done to her because she is in a wheelchair. Some people use "baby talk" when they speak to her, and pat her on the head like she is a three-year-old.

Steve began his session doing a mime. A preacher not using words... interesting. He took a big bag of sugar, wet his finger, dipped it in the bag, and touched his tongue, and smiled. Then, he took a huge spoonful of sugar and shoved it in his mouth, making the crowd cringe. After that, he took a lemon, sliced it in half, licked it, and made the face you are probably making now. Suddenly, with a flick of the wrist, he popped the whole section of lemon in his mouth, making a whole group of pastors squirm in their seats and contort their faces. Finally, he put some sugar and some lemon juice together in a cup and drank it. He made lemonade. His subjects that day were the "Sovereignty of God" and "Man's Free Will"—two opposite truths that alone can bring confusion and strong reactions, but together shed light on some difficult subjects.

The Lord continues to use Joni. Her daily radio show, *Joni and Friends*, gives me a boost every time I hear it. For the last thirty-four years, I have worked at the CADES school in Swarthmore, Pennsylvania. CADES stands for Children and Adult Disability Educational Services. CADES has the most amazing staff, caring for 200 wonderful folks. We have collected used wheelchairs that her "Wheels for the World" program refurbishes and delivers to folks all over the world.

I have had the honor of sharing my comedy program at her family camps. *Joni and Friends* helps parents and caregivers get a much-needed break, and campers with special needs are treated like royalty for a week.

Joni at work.

I WISH I KNEW

Westley:	*What are our liabilities?*
Inigo Montoya:	*There is but one working castle gate, and… and it is guarded by sixty men.*
Westley:	*And our assets?*
Inigo Montoya:	*Your brains, Fezzick's strength, and my steel.*
Westley:	*I mean, if we only had a wheelbarrow. That would be something.*
Inigo Montoya:	*Where did we put that wheelbarrow the albino had?*
Fezzik:	*Over the albino, I think.*
Westley:	*Well, why didn't you list that among our assets in the first place?*

—From *The Princess Bride*

I wish I knew that God doesn't make bad things good, but He can make something good come out of a bad thing. I am not denying pain, but many times we fall victim to the pity party. We cite everything going wrong, and keep a list of everything we don't have or can't do. But Joni's life is one that shouts—no matter what the obstacles are—that we each have some talent or ability that can bless others. So how about you? List your assets! What talent or ability could you use to help someone else? Is there something you learned during a tough time that not only gives you compassion and empathy for others, but something you could share with someone facing something similar?

One of my absolute favorite paintings by Joni.

PART II

COMEDY CONNECTIONS

CHAPTER 14
TAKE ME OUT TO THE BALLGAME!

"You should go to other people's funerals. If you don't, they won't come to yours!"—Yogi Berra

"Why do baseball coaches and managers wear the team uniform during games? Some of these old guys look awful. Just think if they did this in basketball—made the coach wear the uniform. I don't want to think about Spurs Coach Popovich in a uni... and Bill Belichick wearing full Patriots gear? Nobody would listen to him!"—Taylor Mason

"Pete Rose said that the odds of him being reinstated by Major League Baseball are about 7-1."—Jeff Dwoskin

I was fresh out of Williamson trade school, working shiftwork at a Gulf Oil refinery. For fun, I coached a Little League team.

It was time to give back from my vast experience sitting on the bench. The first night of Little League tryouts, all the kids wear numbers, take a few grounders, throw a few balls, and hit a few pitches. The new coaches score them and draft their team. I don't want to get into the politics of Little League sports, but there is a lot. How do the best players always end up on the same team? Rumors of Russian meddling have not been proven, but something is very suspicious. Side note to parents: if you want your kid to play, you better coach. But I had no kids—I just liked sports.

We drafted our teams, I gave a warm welcome and an inspiring talk to my future Hall of Famers. Shirts and caps were handed out to kids with little hands whose baseball mitts weigh as much as they do. As parents picked up their kids, I noticed a big Lincoln Continental, kind of purplish in color, pull up the dirt driveway. As the door opened, I recognized Julie DeJohn immediately. I had seen her on *The Mike Douglas Show* many times. What a voice! She could belt out a Broadway tune or move you to tears with a love song, and the next moment have you on the floor laughing at her comedy. She was a local gal with a national reputation. And her son was on my team. My team!

As the parents collected their kids, I walked over and introduced myself. Told her how much I enjoyed her shows, and kinda mentioned how many folks told me that I ought to get into comedy. Julie was a rare gem who delighted in helping others get started. "I'd love to hear your act. Get me a tape."

Well, I didn't have tape of my act, because I didn't have a tape recorder. Or an act. I did have a ton of funny stories I told at parties while other folks made-out. But I was working now, so off to Radio Shack I went to pay $29.99 for a simple-but-effective recorder, a few more bucks for a three-pack of cassettes, and then off to the basement to record "my best stuff."

A day after giving Julie my cassette, the big star called me. Who does that? She invited me to her house. Who does that? And she met me at the door and handed me back my cassette. Feelings of instant rejection swept over me... until I heard the words, "This is cute!" causing me to smile, soaking in the affirmation. It didn't last long. She calmly continued, "People don't pay for cute!" and another wave of despondency hit me. I can be an emotional rollercoaster. I have more ups and downs then a kangaroo on a pogo stick. "People don't pay for cute" is great advice for all the aspiring comics out there.

"But you have a gift. You have 'IT,'" she said, stressing the word IT. "You are a natural. I like your style, but you need material. Here's what I want you to do: take this one-hour tape with all your stories and get me six good minutes out of it. I want you to get to a punchline every 15-20 seconds. I want you to cut out every unnecessary word. I want you to come see my show and see what I do. And when you have your six minutes down, I'll let you open for me."

Me working with, and learning from, the legendary Julie DeJohn.

Who does that? What did she have to gain? Over the next few months, she met with me, and we would chat after the baseball games. She took me to several shows, big venues like Palumbo's, and local stuff at Catholic churches and town fairs. I watched how she prepared, how she treated the staff, how she interacted with audiences, and noted what got the biggest laughs. Comedy University 101, with a real pro. I was being groomed by one of the greats.

"True, he is no Prince Charming, but there is something in him I simply didn't see."—From *Beauty and the Beast*

"The things that make me different, are the things that make me—me!"—Piglet in *Winnie the Pooh*

Two thoughts. First, we need to be able to identify our own strengths. Jason DeMers, in an article titled "Traits That Only Happy People Have", listed self-confidence as a key. Each of us has gifts, abilities, and passions. Becoming aware of them is vital. Second, happy, successful people are not threatened by, or jealous of, other's success. In fact, it makes them happier when they can help others succeed. I am eternally grateful for what Julie DeJohn did for me, and thrilled to have a small part in mentoring some really funny guys like Ryan Bomgarner, Clay Cox, and Al Smith, and funny gals like Rhonda Corey, and Sandi Joy!

CHAPTER 15
BRAIN FREEZE

Panel One: Charlie Brown says, "Look at those clouds, Linus and Lucy." Panel Two: Lucy says, "I see a map showing the coastline of British Honduras in the Caribbean. Panel Three: Linus says, "I see the profile of Thomas Eakins, the famous artist and sculptor, and over there is the scene in the Bible where Steven is being stoned. What do you see, Charlie Brown?" Panel Four: Charlie Brown says, "I was going to say a horsey and a ducky, but I changed my mind."—From *Peanuts* by Charles Schulz

"I am writing a book. So far, I have the page numbers done."

"I hate it when my leg falls asleep because I know it will be up all night."

"I busted a mirror, which should bring seven years bad luck, but my lawyer thinks he can get me five."

"I have the world's largest collection of sea shells. I keep it at the beach. Perhaps you've seen it?"—Steven Wright

"According to most studies, people's number one fear is public speaking. Number two is death. Death is number two. Does that sound right? This means to the average person, if you go to a funeral, you're better off in the casket than doing the eulogy."
—Jerry Seinfeld

"I think you're ready," Julie said. "There is a special event coming up in a few weeks—Rudy Pompilli Night!!" Who in the world is Rudy Pompilli? I didn't know, and I'm from here. But I did know about Bill Haley & His Comets, whose song *(We're Gonna) Rock Around the Clock* was number one for eight weeks, and was later the theme song for *Happy Days*. Bill Haley and Julie DeJohn grew up right in my area—Chester, Pennsylvania. Folks who put the blue in blue collar. Rudy, the Comets' saxophone player, had passed away and apparently left some money in his will to have a party in his honor. A party to entertain other entertainers. Since he spent his whole life entertaining others, he wanted entertainers to have a special night just for them. It was held at the Nite Cap Lounge in Chichester, right off Exit 2 on I-95.

By eight o'clock, the place was packed. Several talented '50s-style bands, like the J's, filled the room with those golden oldies. Every half hour a bell rang, and the bartender would shout, "Drinks are on Rudy!" And folks would fill up their glasses, lift up their bottles, and offer a toast to Rudy. I walked around with my white leisure suit and bright red tulip shirt

JULIE DeJOHN   GORDY DOUGLAS

FEBRUARY 3, 1977   8 PM 'TIL 2 AM

THE NITE CAP LOUNGE, 1919 Chichester Ave., Boothwyn, Pa.

PRESENTS — A MEMORIAL TRIBUTE TO **RUDY POMPILII**

CONTINUOUS ENTERTAINMENT
Starring

Julie DeJohn   Gordy Douglas

Music By

The Happy Days   &   The Crestmen

Many Surprise Guests

Tickets On Sale Now

THE CRESTMEN   THE HAPPY DAYS

My very first show, as "Gordy" Douglas.

(I still have it). There were all kinds of local leaders and entertainers filling the place. I recognized a lot of them. My first show was in front of professional entertainers. I hadn't even been on stage since the 8th grade, when I made the whole school laugh. I didn't work my way up through comedy clubs because there were very few comedy clubs. There were nice clubs, and nightclubs, and theaters, and restaurants. With Julie's help, I was starting at the top!

I went from the bathroom to the back room again and again, going over my lines, then having to "go again," if you know what I mean. The night before, I stood on the top of oil tanks on the midnight shift at the refinery practicing every word in every joke, I had it memorized, but was I ready? Then it happened. The band stopped, and so did my heart. I heard the host say, "Ladies and gentlemen, we have a special guest tonight, a young comedian making his debut. Welcome to the stage, GORDY DOUGLAS!"

I walked to the small stage where the band still sat. The spotlight hit me in the face, and I could barely see. My heart started pounding so hard I could feel it bursting through my chest. My mouth was dry, and I didn't know how it was possible, but I had to go to the bathroom again… bad.

Looking out, I saw faces of famous people, and some friends who came out to encourage me. I swallowed and began to speak. "Thank you. It is such an honor to be here…" So far, so good. Start humble. "…to do my first show, honoring an award-winning songwriter, an international celebrity..." No problems yet, but then I stopped, mid-sentence. I stared, frozen.... OH, NO! I forgot his name. You know, the guy who died. The guy who died, and folks were here to honor. The guy who left money in his will to make this night possible. The one the whole audience came out to remember. Yes, that guy. I forgot his name; a complete blank. I stood staring at the spotlight, wishing it was a train. *Just kill me now, I'm blowing it.*

I'm not sure how long I was silent. You know me and time. It seemed like five hours; it was probably five seconds. There was a long moment of silence as the crowd stared at me, and I stared back. Then it came to me. I didn't remember his name, but I remembered there was a big poster with his picture and name on the curtain right behind me.

So, I turned real slow and read it... "RUUUUDY... POMMMMMPILLIIIII!" And they roared. It is hard to describe how good laughter feels, but they laughed—a big, loud belly laugh. WOW, this was awesome. I relaxed, just a little. And then I heard these two guys sitting about four feet from me say, "This kid's got chutzpah. He's busting on Rudy!" And I laughed, and they laughed, and I did my six minutes, running off the stage to the bathroom to applause. To quote Sally Fields, "They liked me. They really, really liked me." I couldn't wait to do it again.

And with Julie's help, I did do it again. She took me to a few shows, including some talent shows she hosted to raise money for the Brandywine Youth Club, our local Little League. She took the *Julie and Friends Show* to Rose Tree Park in nearby Media, where "we" performed for over 2,000 people.

And the rest, they say, is history. I am not sure what Julie heard on that little cassette tape, but she saw something, heard something, and was willing to help. And when I got my first big chance, I almost blew it.

Me doing it again—opening for the great Julie DeJohn.

I WISH I KNEW

To do what you love most, you may have to do what you dread most."—Bruce Wilkerson in *The Dreamgiver*

I wish I knew that most folks want to laugh, and want you to succeed. Most of my fears are not based on reality. And even if they were, so what? What is the worst that can happen if you tried to follow your dream? Comedian Steven Wright, whose slow delivery started with a Brain Freeze, said, "I've always had to conquer fear when I'm on stage. Basically, I was, and still am, a very shy person. It's absolutely in conflict with what I do. But once I deliver the first joke, I'm okay." What fear is holding you back? In the words of Yoda from *Star Wars*, "DO or DO NOT. There is no try!"

"The human brain starts working the moment you are born and never stops until you stand up to speak in public."—George Jessel

CHAPTER 16
THE GREAT ESCAPE

I am riding home on the train, sitting on a newspaper, and some guy comes up and says 'Are you reading that?' I said, 'Yes!' and stood up, turned the page, and sat down again."

"Growing up, my nose was so big, I thought it was a third arm. I kept waiting for a hand and fingers to form."

"I grew up in a tough part of Philadelphia. I went to a bar once and asked, 'What do you have on ice?' And the bartender said, 'You wouldn't know him.'"—David Brenner

"Married men live longer than single men. But married men are a lot more willing to die."

"If life was fair, Elvis would be alive and all the impersonators would be dead."—Johnny Carson

After graduating from Williamson's carpentry shop, I did the logical thing: I went to work in a power plant for Gulf Oil. My dad worked in a refinery, and he assured me that people would always need oil, and there was good security working for a big company. It sounded good, and they were offering $7.42 an hour, almost $2 more than most carpenters in our area. So, I entered the world of electric and steam, filled with pumps, pipes, and pliers.

Most of the crew were grizzled veterans, many from World War II, a couple of men from Korea, and a few younger guys just home from Vietnam. They were a real mix of South Philly Irish and Italians. The old-timers had been "making steam" for thirty-plus years, and not many of them liked it. They did it because it paid good, and you did what you had to do. On the long nightshifts, they would tell stories of the war, planning where they were going on vacation, and dreams of retirement in just a few more years. There was a deep longing to get out!

To escape the heat and the noise, our crew of six ate in the control room and hung out between rounds of checking pumps, temperatures, pressures, and fluid levels. One day at lunch, one of the guys said, "Hey, Gordy, look at this!" He handed me the "entertainment section" of the paper. Reading a paper was how we got our news back then. We would devour the paper, read the sports and comics first, then solve the crossword puzzle and cryptogram before scouring every page. That day, the paper said that *The Mike Douglas Show* was having auditions for a David Brenner look-a-like contest.

We grew up watching *Mike Douglas*. It would be on when we got home from school, just after my mother's favorite soap operas, like *The Edge of Night* and *As the World Turns*. When the biggest names in show business made it to the East Coast, they made an appearance on Mike Douglas to plug a book or promote a movie.

Almost daily folks will ask me, "Do you know who you look like?" As a comedian, I quickly respond with "Brad Pitt or Hulk Hogan." It always gets a laugh. One of my co-workers said, "Gordy, you ought to do this. You look like David Brenner!" A tall, thin guy with a long, sharp nose from South Philly, this was a shoo-in. How many guys like that could there be? Scanning the paper for more info, my heart sank. "Rats! The auditions are today." Worse than that, they were in two hours! There was no way I could make it. I was stuck at work, and you just don't "slip away" from a refinery. OR COULD YOU?

Being on a show like *Mike Douglas* could launch a career. It had a national audience. This was the chance of a lifetime, but what could I do? I was stuck at a job I hated, with a crew of some of the roughest, toughest, salt-of-the-earth, blue-collar men God ever created. Men like "Lukey." Lukey was one of the oldest guys there, and he walked with a big limp, like the old cowboy actor Walter Brennan in *Rio Bravo*. Not sure if it

Comedian David Brenner is at Palumbo's through Sept. 23.

Me trying to look like David Brenner. I guess it's another Can You Spot the Differences picture!

was from the war or not—you didn't ask Lukey questions. You left him alone. His hands were as big as a catcher's mitt. Lukey loved this job and hated people. Maybe it was the pain in his hip, or memories of the war, or growing up on a farm in the Deep South, but Lukey didn't smile much.

I was near tears when I realized that this carrot dangling in front of me was too far out of reach. I had been doing some shows, and getting some good press, but I felt trapped in the refinery with no way out. As the whistle blew and lunch ended,

I heard, "Hey, kid! Come here!" Lukey gave me a nod that meant come over here, NOW! I slinked over, wondering what I did wrong this time. He said in a low voice, "You need to get to that audition." He looked around and said quietly. "I'll cover for you. Now, get out of here, and hurry back!" And off I flew. Over the pipes and down the steel catwalk to hop in my '71 Mustang fastback, parked under the Penrose Bridge.

I raced downtown into Center City, and after a few wrong turns, I found a parking spot. No coins for the meter, but that didn't stop me. Sprinting a few blocks to 4th and Arch, right across from the Liberty Bell, and one block from Independence Hall, stood KYW studios.

The line was already forming. There was some guy with a clipboard yelling, "If you are here for the David Brenner contest, sign up here!" There were maybe thirty people in line. Some short, some fat, some blond, some women... most looked nothing like David Brenner. But that wouldn't stop anyone from trying to get on TV. Getting on a local show like *Al Alberts Showcase* was monumental. Al and his wife, Stella, had a Saturday morning show that gave young singers and dancers a chance to be with the former singer of The Four Aces.

But that was a local show. To get on *The Mike Douglas Show*, well, people would talk about that for years. It was a sign you had "made it" (even if it was just a contest). We were ushered into the studio with all the lights and cameras and about

100 seats. It seemed so much bigger on TV. We were asked a few questions in front of some of the crew, and then told to leave. They would get back to us. Classic… "Don't call us, we'll call you!"

I came with jokes to tell, and knowing a lot of David Brenner's jokes, I was prepared to use them. Okay, confession time. I did use some of them. I was ready for an audition, but this was not a showcase. It was a lookalike contest.

Rushing back to the refinery, I whispered a "Thank you" to Lukey, who acted like he didn't see me, and didn't know what I was talking about. Back to work I went, cleaning the burners and checking the pumps. A few hours later, the phone in the control room rang. "YO, GORDY! Your mom is on the phone!" She never called me at work. My mom loved to see her kids succeed and gushed, "Some guy from KYW said you are a finalist for some contest, and you need to be at the studio for taping in three days. What is he talking about?"

Jumping and yelling like we did when the Flyers won the Stanley Cup, I got the attention of my crew. I was going to be on *Mike Douglas*! After pats on the back and some needling from the guys about make-up and "Don't forget us when you're famous," I saw Lukey, who just gave me a little nod and walked away.

Three days to prepare. Wanting to stand out and be remembered, I went to Sears and talked them into lending me a tux with the promise that I would mention them "on the air." And they agreed. I made a big wooden medallion of David Brenner's profile and put it on a chain for around my neck. I had seen David Brenner perform many times. He was always well-dressed, and did a clean show. He went on to host *The Tonight Show Starring Johnny Carson* seventy-five times. So, I tried to imitate him. Then, an agent told me, "Gordon, we only need one David Brenner. You will never get anywhere in this business trying to be someone else. Just be yourself!" That is great advice to us all.

So, I had a few of my best jokes ready, with the hopes and prayers I would get a chance to talk.

The day of the taping, one of the five finalists was getting high back stage. Melvin Belli, the famous lawyer who was once Jack Ruby's lawyer, was the main guest. Mel Tillis, known for his stuttering as much as his singing, was the musical guest. He has a show in Branson now, and get this, his backup singers are called The Stutterettes! In the green room, David Brenner sat there with a beautiful girl from Israel at his side. On the monitor, before flatscreen TV's, we watched Melvin discuss his current trial, a break for commercial, then David came out and did a few jokes, and then we went to commercial again.

When we were given the cue that the show was back on the air in 5-4-3-2-1, Mike told the audience about the contest, as he and David stood center stage. Five of us were marched out and stood in a line. The first guy looked more like Cary

Grant than David Brenner. David got a big laugh when he put his arm around the guy and said, "Look at us, we're dead ringers!" There was nothing special about the next guy, and then they came to me.

"Tell us who you are, and something about yourself."

"Well, my name is Gordon Douglas." And before I could get out the next line, the audience gave out an "Ooooh," sensing this contest might be "fixed." You know, a "Douglas" family contest.

Mike immediately got defensive and said, "No, NO, we are not related—are we, Gordon?"

Without a blink, I put my arm around him and said, "Not if you say so, Uncle Mike!" and the crowd roared. Host Mike Douglas laughed, too, and asked me, "So, what do you do?"

"I'm a comedian working with Julie DeJohn."

"Oh, we love Julie. Send her our love."

I continued to crack jokes about my tux and something about hush puppies. The crowd laughed.

The next two contestants didn't get near the time I did. Soon, the audience was asked to applaud for the contestant who looked most like David Brenner. Mike held his hand over each head, and the audience clapped politely. I got a nice round of applause, but when the hand went over contestant number four, the crowd erupted. Found out later, his family had gotten thirty tickets to the show and stacked the audience. Ah, show business and politics.

When the show aired, most of my brilliant comedy was not shown. They kept the line about "Uncle Mike" and the hushpuppies, but nothing else. Julie called because I told her how I gave her a plug, and she didn't hear it. "I think I know what happened," she said. "You got more laughs than the star, and they cut it out. You can't make the star look bad." I'm not sure that's what happened, but for the next twenty years, people in my little town knew me as the "guy who was on *The Mike Douglas Show*."

All this happened because of Lukey. I heard that he died three months after retiring. He may never have gotten out, but he sure helped me.

"As soon as you pursue a dream, your life wakes up, and everything has meaning."—Barbara Sher

Radical thought—could you fulfill your dream in the job you now have? I hated the refinery. I took the job because it paid better than anything else, and my dad thought it was big having the security of a big oil company. But

> *Never give up on what you really want to do. The person with a big dream is more powerful than the one with all the facts!*—Albert Einstein

I was getting depressed, actually sick, and desperately wanted out, as my dream continued to grow. I'm a blue-collar guy,

115

so this dream seemed ridiculous. Sure, I was having fun, but could you actually make a living at this?

Comedy genius Jim Carrey spoke at a graduation at Maharishi University in Iowa. He said, with great emotion, "So many of us chose our path out of fear disguised as practicality. What we really want seems impossibly out of reach and ridiculous to expect, so we never dare to ask the universe for it. I'm saying: I'm the proof that you can ask the universe for it.

"My father could have been a great comedian, but he didn't believe that was possible for him. So, he made a conservative choice. Instead, he got a safe job as an accountant, and when I was twelve years old, he was let go from that safe job and our family had to do whatever we could to survive.

"I learned many great lessons from my father, not the least of which was that you can fail at what you don't want, so you might as well take a chance on doing what you love."

CHAPTER 17
THE GONG SHOW

Bob Wiley (played by Bill Murray) [Speaking to workers in a mental hospital]: It reminds me of my favorite poem, which is, "Roses are red, violets are blue, I'm a schizophrenic... and so am I."

Bob Wiley [telling a joke]: The doctor draws two circles and says, "What do you see?" The guy says, "Sex."
[Everybody laughs.]
Bob Wiley: Wait a minute, I haven't even told the joke yet! So, the doctor draws trees. "What do you see?" The guy says, "Sex." The doctor draws a car, owl... "Sex, sex, sex." The doctor says to him. "You are obsessed with sex." He replies, "Well, you're the one drawing all the dirty pictures!"
—From *What About Bob?*

"I went to a Hollywood party the other day. Wilt Chamberlain was there. I couldn't resist. I asked him, 'How is the weather up there?' He said, 'It's raining,' and he spit on me."

"I took my dog to a flea party, and he stole the show."
—Murray Langston as The Unknown Comic on *The Gong Show.*

"You know, you can't please all the people all the time. And last night, all those people were at my show."—Mitch Hedberg

The world was changing. Television was changing. Three channels were now joined by UHF, where every afternoon you could watch cartoons like *Speed Racer, Astro Boy, 8th Man,* and *Marine Boy.* Monday night had wrestling, with heroes like Haystacks Calhoun and Bruno Samartino. Today, we have *America's Got Talent,* or *The Voice,* or *Dancing with the Stars.* In my day, there was *The Gong Show.* Singers, dancers, animal acts, and comedians all trying to get through their ninety seconds without the celebrity judges picking up the giant hammer and hitting the eight-foot cymbal behind them. Crowds were like sharks smelling blood. One bad note, one mistake, one bad joke, and the chants would start: "GONG HIM! GONG HIM!"

There were very few comedy clubs in the '70s. A few in New York, like Catch a Rising Star, or The Comedy Store in L.A. There was one in the Olde City part of Philly—Grandmom Minnie's on 2nd Street. They were having a talent show. A homemade "Gong Show." It wasn't far from Christ Church where George Washington attended (and just around the corner from Ben Franklin's home). Given what that city was up against, I guess a place to pray might come in handy. Anyway, Philly has such great history, both for our country and comedy.

A contest, against amateurs? This should be easy. It was my first show on my own, without Julie. I was act thirty-eight out of forty, which meant I would get on stage somewhere around midnight. There were a few good singers and a few bad ones, and some really bad ones that got the crowd chanting, "GONG THEM! GONG THEM!" There were three local celebrity judges, including comic Stewie Stone. It was getting late; people were tired. Most of the crowd was made up of friends of the other acts. They came to support their friends, and now that their friends had done their thing, they were long gone, and the judges wanted to join them.

Just before I got on stage, three adorable triplets, about fifteen years old and wearing identical dresses, took the stage. They would have been perfect for *The Lawrence Welk Show*, not a comedy club at midnight. Their "show business mother" exhorting her girls to, "Sing, girls. Aren't they beautiful?" trying to get some crowd support. You could see the terror in the young girls' eyes. Their fluffy dresses couldn't hide their shaking knees. Three notes in and that rock-'n-roll crowd started booing, and one of the judges reached for the hammer.

Before the first verse of the song was over, the gong sounded. "Keep going, girls!" the mom shouted, and they sang some

119

more. The booing got louder, and so did the mom. "SING, GIRLS, SING! You're doing great!" The girls tried to keep going, but the crowd had voted and they were not going to let anyone ignore "THE GONG." The girls had tears in their eyes, not knowing whether to listen to their mom and keep on singing, or run off the stage. They chose the latter, and the crowd cheered wildly, like they just killed the bull in Spain. There was a group hug as the mom said, "Don't worry, girls, you did great. They don't know real talent when they see it."

The emcee was ready to call it quits. "Next up—we have stand-up comedian Gordon Douglas." He looked at me and shrugged. That was all I had written on the index card. Who knew you were supposed to sell yourself?

I had only done a handful of shows with Julie. Her shows were always packed with folks who loved her and came out to see her. Middle-aged folks with manners. She always gave me this big build-up before bringing me on stage. This was a whole new world for me. I took the stage and grabbed the mic. I had heard that you only get fifteen seconds to win or lose an audience. Julie taught me to start with your best joke and end with your second-best joke, or was it the other way around? But starting strong, and ending stronger, was the key.

The first joke got a little laugh, not a big one. The second joke even less. I could see the guy reaching for the hammer. Panicking, I raced through the third joke and got a laugh, then onto my fourth joke… nothing, they didn't get it, or they didn't care. Before they could gong me, I said, "That's my show. Thanks for hanging around. Enjoy your last two acts." And I ran offstage humbled, thinking, *I'm soooo not ready for this.*

I WISH I KNEW

"Failure is an event, not a person."—Zig Ziglar

"If at first you don't succeed, don't try skydiving!"—Steven Wright

I wish I knew that not every show would be great, and it's good to bomb every now and then. It sure keeps you humble. It is a mystery to me why some jokes get laughs nine shows in a row, but then for some unknown reason, nobody laughs the tenth time. I had been spoiled doing shows with Julie. In baseball, if your batting average is .300, you can be an All-Star, even though it means you did not get a hit seven of the last ten times you got up to bat. That is not a good average for a comedian, though.

Happy people are not surprised by adversity, but accept that sometimes things don't go according to plan. Psychologist Peter Kramer wrote that "Happiness isn't the opposite of depression—resilience is."

Don't let a setback be the end of the line for you. Samuel Beckett said, "Ever tried? Ever failed? No matter. Try again, fail again, fail Better!" Inventor Thomas Edison made one thousand unsuccessful attempts at inventing the light bulb. When a reporter asked him how it felt to fail one thousand times. Edison replied, "I didn't fail a thousand times. The light bulb was invented in one thousand steps."

So, maybe it's time you bounce back and take another step.

CHAPTER 18
HEE HAW

"My first show, there wasn't much laughter, but I did hear one guy clapping loudly! Then I saw him smacking the bottom of a ketchup bottle."—Bob Hope

"UCLA is testing some new medicines on Don Rickles. They want to make sure it is safe for the rats!"—Impressionist Rich Little

Johnny Cash: Hey, Roy, you going to the movies tonight?
Roy Clark: Nah, I ain't going.
Johnny Cash: Now, Roy, that's bad grammar. It's I am not going, you are not going, he is not going. Get it?
Roy Clark: Yeah, ain't nobody going!
—From Hee Haw

The Latin Casino was the biggest theater in the Philly area. All the big names appeared there. Everyone from impressionist Rich Little to singer Jackie Wilson. I learned early on you had to tip the maître d' to get a good seat. If you only slipped him a buck, you would be near the bathroom door. If you were really cheap, like my parents, you could end up next to the kitchen and maybe had to wash dishes. I remember taking a girl named Marsha to see Roy Clark of *Hee Haw* fame. Marsha was a classic South Philly girl: dark hair, middle name of Mary, and a last name with about twenty syllables that ended in "O".

I'm not sure why I took Marsha, except she played hard to get. She wouldn't laugh at my jokes, and she didn't seem impressed with my budding comedy career. The more she acted indifferent, the harder I tried to convince her I was "something special." Somehow, I convinced her to come with me to the Latin Casino to see country music star Roy Clark. It was kind of a date. As we entered, I slipped the guy a $20 bill. Soon, we were sitting at the stage.

And what a show! For two hours, we heard some of the best banjo picking in the world, and laughed as the *Hee Haw* family shared funny and corny stories, and several songs brought a tear to your eye, like Roy's signature *Yesterday*. Marsha seemed to be enjoying it, and was impressed that I spent what was equivalent to four-hours salary on a tip for good seats. The meal was good; the show was better. Afterwards, I asked the guy if I could get backstage and chat with Roy. First, because I had heard that Roy was a "believer," and second, because I wanted to impress Marsha.

"And who are you?" the same maître d' asked.

"I'm a young comedian working with Julie DeJohn, and I was looking for some advice."

Knowing how the game was played, I started to slip him another $20. He waved the money away and said, "Any friend of Julie's is a friend of ours. Come on back." Marsha gave a slight look of approval, like maybe I was worth dating. After knocking on the door to the dressing room, a tired, sweaty Roy Clark cracked the door with a towel wrapped around his neck. After a few whispers, the door opened. I was told by the maître d', "You get five minutes. Don't make me come get you!" I guess I was a friend, but not a close friend.

Roy explained that he had been on the road a spell, and he was meeting his family for the first time in a long time. So, getting right to the point, I asked, "Any advice you could give a young comedian?"

"What did you like best about the show tonight?" he asked. I didn't say the music, as country music wasn't my favorite. But the dueling banjo with the national champion was terrific. Seeing some classic skits like the "Oh that's good, no that's bad" with the *Hee Haw* characters was cool. But hearing the applause and seeing the standing ovation touched a nerve in me. How good must that feel to have folks respond that way? He said, "Gordon, it took thirty years to get here. I've done shows for tiny audiences in barns and farms, and now television shows, and big places like this. But I've learned to do every show for an audience of ONE. No matter how big or small the audience, I ask if what I am doing would make HIM smile. And if I can do that, then I am a happy man."

Great advice for entertainers, particularly those of us who call ourselves "Christian comedians," or "Christian singers," or "writers." Then I looked at Marsha, who I wanted so much to impress, and thought of how much I hungered for the approval of others and longed for the applause that made me feel better about myself. It's taken a few decades and a few hundred shows in nursing homes and Bible camps and church basements for me to learn to seek the approval and applause of that one all-important audience member.

Rick Warren's best-selling book, *The Purpose Driven Life*, rephrased what I learned in catechism class. Translating the first question, "What is the chief end of man?" Rick asks, "What is the main reason we are here?" The answer I learned was to "glorify God and enjoy HIM— forever!" Rick's translation in modern speech: "Let everything you say and do make God smile, and you will enjoy Him, and enjoy life!" Good advice for a great life, whether you are a comedian or not.

Oh, and as for me and Marsha? Never saw her again, but I plan on seeing my "audience of ONE" forever!

I WISH I KNEW

"I may be a big fish in a small pond, but I am a very happy fish."—Dennis Lewis, funny father of Jerry Lewis, responding to his son's requests to get him to join him in performing in bigger venues.

I wish I knew that what we do, and where we do it, is not nearly as important as why we do it, and maybe WHO we do it for. Roy's advice was good. We get caught up in chasing the next big thing. Happy people know they are part of something much bigger than themselves.

CHAPTER 19
VICTORY AT
VALLEY FORGE

Joey Bishop and Sammy Davis, Jr. are speeding down the highway, driving from Las Vegas to L.A. When a cop pulls them over and asks, "Do you know how fast you were driving?" Joey leans over and says, "Officer, he only has one eye. Do you want him looking at the road or the speedometer?"

"A man with a tool belt knocks on the door. A parrot answers. 'Who is it?' 'It's the plumber!' The parrot answers again, 'Who is it? Who is it?' The man answers louder, 'It's the plumber, the plumber!' Silence follows, so the man knocks on the door, and the parrot chirps, 'WHO IS IT? WHO IS IT?' The man yells, 'IT'S THE PLUMBER! THE PLUMBER!' He is so enraged, his blood pressure soars, and he passes out on the sidewalk. A little old lady drives up, gets out of her car, sees the man on the sidewalk and says, 'Oh, my, who is this?' and the bird says... 'It's the plumber, the plumber!'"—Danny Thomas teaching Diana Ross how to tell a joke

"I went to a church in Chicago. Church had six Commandments and four do-the-best-you-cans."

"I was walking around Taiwan and bought some flip-flops for my feet. I said I wonder where they were made? Looked under the bottom. It said, 'Just around the corner.'"—George Wallace

Valley Forge! The words bring to mind a frigid military camp. Who hasn't seen the famous painting of George Washington out in the woods, kneeling in the snow, offering a prayer for his frozen troops? In the 1970's, Valley Forge not only had a national park, it had a theater. A great theater; a theater in the round. Which means the stage was a big circle, and it slowly rotated during the show. Sometimes you see the front, sometimes the "other side." My wife and I went there for our first anniversary to see Tom Jones. Man, that guy can sing. He did all the classics: *What's New Pussycat?, The Green, Green Grass of Home*, and *Delilah*! Yes, women ran up to the stage and threw underwear to Tom. That doesn't happen to comedians. Oh, stuff can get thrown, but it isn't a Cross Your Heart bra. The opening act was comedian George Wallace. That name might not mean much to the younger readers, but there was a politician in the Deep South known for his racism and bigotry. And this comedian, named George Wallace, was black. That is funny, and he was funny. With lines like, "I was so dumb in school, all I got was D's and F's, so I tried to convince my parents it was part of a new grading system. It meant DOING FINE, DOING FINE!"

But two years earlier, two giants of comedy shared that rotating stage together—Joey Bishop and Danny Thomas in one show. I think it was called, *The Legends of Comedy*. Joey was part of the Rat Pack with Sinatra, and guest-hosted *The Tonight Show* more than anyone else. Danny Thomas was a master of dialects. He told stories with an Italian accent, or an Irish brogue.

So, there I was in the parking lot for the first night of a week-long engagement. I got there two hours early, and sat in the parking lot. I saw the limo pull up and go around back, and followed them. As they got out, I jumped out and waved to them as their entourage walked them into the dressing room. I am not sure they even saw me. I bought my ticket, went into the theater, and laughed at every line.

The show featured other acts. A janitor who was mopping the stage bumps the mic, then starts singing in this amazing operatic voice. A husband-and-wife gymnastics team did their lifts and contortions while Joey Bishop tried to crack them up. All this, and a full orchestra. Great show!

The second night I parked in the back, closer to the dressing room door, and stood and waved as they exited the limo. They saw me; how could they not? Who stands in a parking lot wearing a three-piece suit? They waved back.

The third night, there I stood, leaning on my car. When they got out of the limo, I prayed as I began to wave. Danny Thomas yelled over to me. "Hey, kid, what are you doing here so early every night?" I told him I was a comedian trying to get started and wanted to learn all I could. "Well, come on in," he said without hesitation. The dressing room was filled with maybe six other guys—agents, producers, friends. "So, tell me what you do," Danny said, seemingly genuinely interested.

It didn't take long to recap my two years in show business. I shared a few of my jokes, and they laughed. Joey's agent came over and started asking me what kind of events I did, where I performed, and how long a show I could do—as Danny slipped away. The agent slipped me a card and told me his son was doing some stuff in the Philly area and maybe he could help me out. Then, for the next hour, I sat in the green room and watched two giants prepare.

They swapped stories with me about their early days, best gigs, worst audiences, each one trying to top the other and pouring out such wisdom. They really wanted to help me. The ironing board was up and the tuxes were being neatly pressed. Every show you gotta look your best and do your best!

There was a knock on the door. It opened a crack, and a loud voice yelled, "Ten minutes till curtain!" Danny and Joey (I can call them that now, since we are close) started to get dressed. Right there with everyone milling around. White shirt, fancy ties, looking at their hair and faces in the mirror.

"Five minutes till curtain!" came the voice again. You could hear the orchestra playing when the door opened. Joey was all set and ready to go. Danny was all dressed, except for his pants. There he was in a nice tux... and boxer shorts. Long and slow and quiet, Danny said, "Joooeyyyy! Where did you put my pants?" The agent gave me an elbow and a "watch this" nod of his head.

Joey looked sheepish, shrugged, and gave that, "I don't know what you're talking about" look. Danny opened drawers and closets, to no avail. Then, in a soft voice, Joey said, "You're getting warmer!" Danny stopped and looked at him.

"Two minutes till curtain!" The music was ramping up; the crowd was getting seated. Danny started going in circles... "Warmer, colder, warmer... hotter, hotter, really hot!" said Joey with a smile, and Danny furiously turned over cushions on the couch, peaked into the refrigerator, and found his chilly pants!

The music stopped, and the booming voice of the master of ceremonies said, "Welcome to the Valley Forge Music Fair, where tonight, two of the biggest legends in the world of comedy will share the stage. Ladies and gentlemen, I present to you Joey Bishop and Danny Thomas!"

With the orchestra in full swing, Joey walked out on stage and took bow after bow while Danny rushed to put his newly found pants on. When he stumbled onto the stage, still zipping up, he looked at Joey, and... and... and he laughed. He laughed,

Joey laughed, and the crowd laughed. The first two nights I had watched them enter the stage in different orders and always with some funny expression and big smiles.

"See that, kid?" said the agent. "Thirty years in the business, and they still have fun. They pull tricks on each other every night, so when they go on stage, they are laughing. You know why, kid? 'Cause laughter is contagious, and when they're laughing, the crowd is laughing."

He then handed me a piece of paper. "Danny wanted you to have this." It was a handwritten note, saying:

Dear Gordy, Sorry I couldn't introduce you tonight, but the producer wouldn't allow it. Good Luck.—Danny Thomas

Can you believe it? After my five-minute conversation/ audition, Danny tried to get me on the show. I shared part of a quote by David Letterman earlier. Here is the rest of it: "I have spent a lot of time wondering why I am not happier. I am happiest when I am doing something for someone who can't pay me back!" The greatest legacy of Danny Thomas is not his awards, or record sales, or having his own television show, but St. Jude's Hospital.

"I don't think human beings learn anything without desperation. Desperation is a necessary ingredient to learning anything or creating anything. Period."—Jim Carrey

As a young man, Danny Thomas had a simple goal: to entertain people and be successful enough at it to provide for his wife and family. But work wasn't easy to come by. As he and his family struggled, his despair grew. He wondered if he should give up his dreams of acting and find a steady job. He turned to St. Jude Thaddeus, the patron saint of hopeless causes. "Show me my way in life," he vowed to the saint one night in a Detroit church, "and I will build you a shrine." His prayer was answered, and Danny kept his word, building St. Jude's Hospital. It is worth looking up and reading how the money was raised, and how it was built. You've probably seen the commercials asking you to give. And since the doors opened, no family has ever gotten a bill. That is amazing. And although I am not big on praying to the saints, I have often thought of myself as a hopeless cause. And with the help of Joey Bishop and Danny Thomas, I am so grateful they encouraged me to keep going. "Desperation and Gratitude" make a powerful team.

> *"Cries for help are frequently inaudible."*
> —Tom Robbins, *Even Cowgirls Get the Blues*

CHAPTER 20
GENE PERRET &
CAROL BURNETT

"Hi, Bob 'Mosquito Net' Hope here! What a rough flight on the way here to the South Pacific. I asked the pilot if there were any parachutes. He said, 'Don't be silly. Anyone with a parachute left an hour ago!'"

Bombshell Ursula Andress said, "Bob, you know I can't sing, and I can't dance. What am I doing here?" "You just stand there, and these guys will do the singing and dancing!"—Bob Hope

Snoring is nature's way of saying, "Hey, everybody, look at me, I am sleeping!"—Gene Perret

"I've really been having fun on this trip. Why, just last night, Miss USA asked if I'd mind taking a walk. By the way, what's a plank?"—Bob Hope (written by Martha Bolton)

Charlie Bell was one of the "old-timers" at Gulf Oil, and quite a character. Word on the street was he had done some vaudeville in his day. Every day he came in and told two or three jokes with sound effects. He reminded me of a cross between The Muppets' Fozzie Bear and Charlie Callas. Charlie Callas was one of the few guys who could make my dad laugh out loud. His faces and body contortions, along with foreign dialects and sound effects, made him one of my favorites on television. The first few weeks I worked at the refinery, I thought Charlie Bell was hilarious. His act got a little old after the second month, and by the third, it was wearing thin. It seemed that Charlie only had about ten jokes. Apparently, that was all you needed in vaudeville because you did your show with a cast and then moved on to the next town and the next, so you didn't need new material.

One day, he mentioned he had a connection with Bob Hope. He had gone to school with a guy named Gene Perret, who was now writing for Bob Hope. Charlie thought Gene might be able to help me. Sure, I had heard of Bob Hope, who, for forty-one straight Christmases, went overseas to entertain the troops. We grew up watching his *Road to...* movies and holiday specials. I think of Bob Hope every time I hear the song *Silver Bells*. But Gene Perret? Who was he? I never paid much attention to the names scrolling at the end of the television programs. That was when we raced to get a snack or hit the bathroom. I've since learned that Gene Perret was Bob Hope's lead writer for over twenty years. He also wrote for *The Dean Martin Celebrity Roasts* and for *The Carol Burnett Show*. It doesn't get bigger than that.

So, what did I have to lose? I gave Charlie Bell a cassette recording of my show, along with a letter asking for advice, and honestly, I never expected anything to come of it. You get a lot of promises and rejections in show business, and it's hard not to get cynical. But a few weeks later, I got a six-page, handwritten letter from the one and only Gene Perret.

He encouraged me, he corrected me, he taught me, and he teamed me up with a young writer named Bob Mills. And get this, he invited me to California. There were some auditions going on, and he said if I was in the area, he'd be glad to take me to lunch and show me around. We corresponded a few more times, and I took my two-week vacation from the refinery in Philly, and headed to Hollywood.

We met for lunch at Benihana's, his treat. He gave me a personal tour through CBS Studios. I saw all kinds of celebrities, including Mary Tyler Moore, walking in the hallways. I sat in on tapings of *The Dinah Shore Show* and *The Tonight Show*. The band under Doc Severinsen was amazing before the show, and during commercials. Things you don't see or hear at home.

I went to The Comedy Store every night to watch rising starts like Robin Williams, Jimmie "J.J." Walker, Ellen DeGeneres, and Jay Leno. Most nights, the emcee was a wise-cracking, gap-toothed comedian named David Letterman, who roasted me one night for starting the oil crisis. The level of talent was huge. Many, like Elayne Boosler and George Miller, were equally good, though not as well-known. They could hold their own with any comedian out there. George wore a Mister Rogers type sweater, and with a somewhat mousy voice said, "I don't think I should trust my dentist. He sells miniature ivory chess sets in the lobby." What had I gotten into?

Gene told me about some kind of open-mic audition. Word was, they were looking for some comedians to be on *American Bandstand*, and network scouts would be there. I signed up and went, and did something I regret to this day. I should say I didn't do something. I didn't go on stage. I chickened out. Seeing that level of talent, I just didn't think I was ready, and when they called my name, I didn't go up. Years have passed, and I've learned it is better to go on with the big guns. Many times the laughter is going so strong, the audience carries you. But fear got the better of me.

I lacked a few things, and confidence was at the top of the list. You only get that after a few hundred shows. What is that adage? Doing something 10,000 times makes you a pro? I was more than 9,900 shows short. I also lacked a polished fifteen minutes of material. But I still had a dream of being discovered, and I still believed in miracles. My newfound faith in God, and all the doors that continue to open for me so far, had me believing that the Lord had great things in mind for me. But that didn't mean it would be easy, and I didn't have to work. My mom used to say "God helps those who help themselves!" Though that is not in the *Bible*, there is some truth to it. He also helps those who can't help themselves. But that doesn't mean we do nothing. Singer Keith Green said it best: "You keep doing your best, pray that it's blest, and He'll take care of the rest!"

My vacation days were running out, but I still had one more chance. There was still hope for me to be discovered and skyrocket to the top. There were reserved tickets to *The Carol Burnett Show* waiting for me, courtesy of Gene. He had given me the tour, taught me how the writers meet and go over stuff with the cast, and then do a rehearsal in front of a live audience earlier in the day. They then go back and tweak the script to get more laughs. I learned that Tim Conway would always do things perfectly in the dress rehearsal, then, when the show was "live," he would improvise and crack up the cast, getting some of the biggest laughs in TV history.

Folks waited in lines for hours in the California heat to get to see a taping of *The Carol Burnett Show*. I arrived a little before showtime and got escorted by a page to center stage, three rows back. Carol came out to thunderous applause, and asked for the houselights to be turned on. Many of her shows began with this fresh, unscripted interaction with the audience, and I was ready. I had my blue three-piece suit on with paisley shirt and no tie. I had some jokes ready, if she called me up on stage. I had seen guys go up and get a kiss, or sing a song with Carol, and I wanted to be the first to go up and tell a few jokes. Who knew? Maybe I could be part of the cast like Vicki Lawrence. A local schoolgirl who had written to Carol invited her to her school. Carol not only went, she helped Vicki become a star.

My hand was raised high and my butt raised off the seat when she asked for questions. I can't remember if I was the first, or the second, but she had this enormous grin and pointed at me with a little nod of her head. "Hi, Carol. I wonder if you have any advice for a young comedian who wants to entertain families?" *Wow, I did it! I am in Hollywood, at a live taping of The Carol Burnett Show, and she called on me, and I am on television right now!!!* I was getting ready to slide down the aisle and come join her on stage, just the way I dreamed it. And Carol quipped, "Sure. Go door to door and tell jokes!" and the crowd roared. It is pretty funny. How do you entertain families? Go door to door and tell jokes. I get it. But that wasn't the way I dreamed it.

I slowly sat down and settled back in my seat. As the laughter subsided, and before she took the next question, she glanced back to me and mouthed the words, "Don't give up!"

It wasn't the thrill of a kiss, or a chance to be on stage, but it sure is good advice. I was more than disappointed, of course. But with a show and a cast like this, who could stay sad long? Between scenes and set changes, when most celebrities run to their dressing rooms or private trailers, the cast mingled with the audience. Dick Van Dyke did a little soft shoe and asked people where they were from. I am still impressed by how nice the whole group was.

I remember buying a postcard and sending it home, saying, *"I will be home soon. Hollywood isn't ready for me, yet!"* Truth is, I wasn't ready for Hollywood. As I later learned, God had a little different plan for me. While so many folks I saw at The Comedy Store ended up on television shows, even getting their own shows, I would spend the next ten years doing something very different. I could learn a thing or two from Charlie Bell. Maybe it takes a few years to get those jokes down perfectly. But thanks to Charlie, I got the trip of a lifetime, and thanks to Gene and Carol, I didn't give up.

It would be years before my comedy career took off. When it did, I met Martha Bolton, one of the top comedy writers in the country, who also worked with Gene Perret cranking out one-liners for Bob Hope. Martha Bolton was teaching a comedy writing class in New York City, with Donna East. It is where we first met. Martha is now writing plays and books like *Don't Ask Delilah for a Trim*, and *Growing Your Own Turtleneck!* Somehow, I keep running into folks who are the best in the business.

My dad and my father-in-law each served our country, and watching Bob Hope specials was a big part of my childhood.

It has been an honor for me to do some events for our military, and I'd love to do more. Speaking of more, you'll see Tommy Moore's name on at least a dozen jokes in this book. Tommy went to Germany, Iceland, England, Belgium, and the Netherlands in 1993 with the Department of Defense. He's another family comedian like me. If you get a chance to see his act someday, do it. It's a throwback to the grand old days of the Catskills. There's just nothing quite like it anymore.

After 911, my wife and I started Operation Bellylaughs, sending comedy tapes and DVDs to the men and women serving in the military. It is our little salute to Bob Hope. I've been able to do a few things for the troops, and am still looking for ways to get on more military bases. When people are willing to make the biggest sacrifice for you, you can never do enough for them.

I WISH I KNEW

The destination is the journey!"—John Wimber

Wimber's quote confused me for years. My focus was on the goal, the prize, making it BIG, proving to all my doubters that I was somebody special. I didn't know I was already special, and you are, too. There is an old Yiddish proverb: "If you want to make God laugh, tell Him your plans." I really thought I could go to Hollywood, appear at a place or two, be discovered, get my own show, and be set for life. My focus was on the goal, not the journey. I wish I knew that I should enjoy the process, and take joy in the journey. Don't look for happiness around the corner—look for it right where you are.

Oh, and if you need a laugh, watch an old Carol Burnett show. They are as funny as ever. Or look up Bob Hope's military tours on YouTube. If you love old-time comedy, or just need more laughter in your life, please read Tommy Moore's *A Ph.D. in Happiness from the Great Comedians*. I have read it at least twenty times. It's a classic.

PART III

CROSS TRAINING

PART III

CROSS TRAINING

CHAPTER 21
BUMPER STICKERS

*"If you have a bumper sticker that says 'God Is My Co-Pilot!',
maybe you ought to switch seats!"*—Brad Stine

*"Warning! In case of Rapture, car will swerve as my mother-in-
law takes the wheel!"*—Mike Williams

"Don't step in my exhaust!"—Seen on the back of an Amish
Buggie

Can you complete these slogans? "Trix are for _____."
"Maxwell House—good to the _____ _____." "Sometimes
you feel like a nut!" exclaimed the commercial for (I bet you
can name that candy bar). How about these candies? Can you
name them, too? "Gimme a break, gimme a break, break me
off a piece of that _____ _____ bar."

How many licks did the owl say it took to get to the center of the _____ _____?

If you're hungry, the commercial blasted, "Grab a_____."

Almond Joy, Kit Kat bars, Tootsie Pops, and Snickers all had catch phrases. Short phrases can be catchy, easy to memorize, and carry a lot of meaning.

Can we reduce a life philosophy down to a few words? I remember the popular 'I FOUND IT' campaign in the '70s. The words stood out on bright yellow bumper stickers. Curious folks were supposed to ask you what you found. Then you could tell them about Jesus. There was a blue bumper sticker that said, "God Loves You, and has a wonderful plan for your life." Many a TV preacher took that idea and promoted to millions of gullible followers that if you just say a certain prayer and stand in faith, you can have a bigger car, a nicer house, a thicker head of hair, and a nicer spouse. They said if you can "Blab it, you can grab it!" "Believe it and receive it!" Declare God's goodness over your life, and you will never have a problem.

And you might just get an extra blessing if you send a check to them. I don't seem to remember Jesus offering that. Ever wonder if they have preachers like that in China, or Turkey, or Syria, where Christians are captured, tortured, and even die for their faith? Now, I am not denying that there is power in our tongue. What we say about ourselves and our lives does make a difference. For more than a year, my wife and I have begun our day by reading out loud things the *Bible* says are true of us. Things like "I am completely forgiven," "I am loved," "My God is for me, so nothing can be against me!" (See Appendix for more.)

There is actual medical proof that what we think and speak about can affect our brain and moods. What I struggle with is taking this idea too far. I don't believe that if we do everything right, or believe something hard enough, we will have no problems, sickness, or pain. Do you know anyone who does?

The *Bible* clearly teaches that God has a plan for each of His children, and for this world. The Apostle Paul wrote to the Church in Ephesus 2:10, "For we are God's workmanship, created in Christ Jesus to do good works, which God prepared in advance for us to do!"

Looking back over fifty years, the happiest, most joy-filled people I know are those who have found out what that plan is and are doing it. And some of the most miserable folks I know have big houses, nice cars, and make a lot more money than I do. So many people are miserable at work and at home and live for the next weekend, so they can PARTY!! There has to be something better. I don't want this book to be preachy, but since you've read this far, you now know that my relationship with God has become the most important thing in my life, though that relationship has been tried and tested many times. It is usually when stuff happens that is not so wonderful. Financial struggles, not seeing victory over bad habits, and sickness and pain all make me ask, "Where is the wonderful life?"

How do you define SUCCESS? How would you complete the sentence, "I am happiest when _____?"

After many years, here's what I've come up with.

Success is… being where God wants you to be, doing what God called you to do, at the right time (and with the right attitude!).

Long before Joel Osteen was on TV, my youth group wrote these words on a sheet:

> *We are WHO the Bible says we are*
> *We have WHAT the Bible says we have*
> *We can do WHATEVER God calls us to do!*

It took me a while to learn that. Back in 1978, I was a young man, fresh out of school, driving a nice, 1971 Ford Mustang and making money. Since graduating, I had pretty much done what I wanted. Some good, some bad. Because I had prayed that special prayer, I believed I already had "my ticket to heaven." So, until God called me home, I wanted to do my own thing.

God had other plans.

It had been three years since I prayed that prayer for forgiveness, and for the next year and a half, I was very active in the daily chapels at Williamson. Yes, daily chapels. Every morning at 7:30, I volunteered to do the Scripture reading, or share a story of how my life was changing, or give a lesson from the *Bible* with five-minute sermonettes. It was great training for public speaking and sharing my faith. I had 200 fellow students watching. Well, not all were watching, or listening— many of them slept. But some took a close look to see if this change in me would last. And sadly, my excessive zeal and limited knowledge turned more than a few off.

Some of the students invited me to go drinking in New Jersey, where the legal age had just been lowered to eighteen. I declined. "You don't have to drink. Just hang out with us," they said. It seemed they had it as their goal to get me to drink or cuss, or fail in some way. There was lots of pressure to lower my standards. "So, you think you're better than us?" "Come on, be a man!" They even tried "Jesus went to weddings and drank wine, so why won't you?" There was incredible pressure to compromise on the outside and a deep longing to fit in on the inside. And I still had a lot of growing up to do. Being teased is tough at any age. It didn't take long for me to learn that it was far better for me when I avoided those situations completely. At this point in my life, I didn't know that your own strength only allows you to resist temptation for a short time. There were a lot of things I needed to learn about myself, and what the *Bible* says about how to win the battles against our own desires, the pressures of the world, and the powers of darkness.

Things can change quickly, particularly when you get

151

separated from the things and people that help you the most. After graduating from Williamson, I started missing going to church. Working shift work and weekends made it hard to make a Sunday morning service. And my college friends from Grace Chapel had moved on with life. Comedy became my focus, and took up much of my spare time, taking me to places I once spent a lot of time and effort trying to avoid. And there was a real emptiness in those places—an emptiness that matched my heart. Oh, I loved the applause and attention, but I craved something more.

After my very short stint in Hollywood, I stayed away from church for a year or two. Then, new doors opened for me. Not doors to comedy clubs or big shows. Invitations came in to speak with teens and churches, including a chance to connect with a new group of college kids and young adults. I resisted for a few months, but constant invitations from my friend, Bill Baillie, wore me down. It only took one meeting for the embers in my heart to stir. I am not sure if it was the singing, or the teaching, or the love this group had for each other, but I couldn't wait till the next meeting.

I began doing some speaking and teaching, and I loved it. Other church groups invited me to speak. They liked hearing the funny guy who found God, though, in truth, the bumper sticker had it wrong. I didn't find God—God sought me, pursued me. And I loved sharing my story. Combining fun and faith came easy. My love of God and love of laughter blended together nicely.

Someone gave me a cassette of Howard Hendrix, a teacher at Dallas Theological Seminary. Although living in Texas, he was originally a Philly guy with a quick wit and a tremendous gift for teaching. The tape was titled *Spiritual M & M's: The Three Most Important Questions in Life*. As a student, I learned to listen for key words and phrases that might be on a test, and this sounded important.

The three questions were:

- Who is my Master?
- What is my Mission?
- Who should be my Mate?

"You don't want to get any of these questions wrong," he said. The consequences are terrible. So, get them right.

Who is my Master? Well, who is in charge of your life? A popular bumper sticker used to say, GOD IS MY CO-PILOT! Comedian Brad Stine said, "If God is your co-pilot, you better switch seats. God is not into riding shotgun!" I knew Jesus as my Savior, but not much was said back then about Jesus also being LORD.

Jesus is not here to serve me—He is also known as the BOSS, KING, LEADER. Jesus didn't come to help me live my life, He came to take over. What? This was a truth I wrestled with and resisted for a few more years. Wasted years. I found out if you fight with God, you lose. Even if God lets you win, you lose. Think about that. Life is so much better when God is in charge, but we will never surrender control of our lives without being totally convinced of His Love. And that took some time for me. I had some healing to do and lessons to learn. I guess I figured I wasn't going down without a fight. Well, I put up a fight, but like I said, I was destined to lose, and by losing to God, I won. I gave my life over to Him.

But what about that next question? What is my Mission? Does my life have purpose? A plan? Is there a reason I am on this earth? Rick Warren wrote about this in *The Purpose Driven Life*. Why? Because there is a deep need in every heart to know my life counts. I have a whole talk centered on finding your CALLING and pursuing your dream. A recent Gallup poll said that more than 70% of people hate their job, which is tragic. (See Appendix for an overview on some key steps on how to confirm your calling.)

Now, for the next most important question. Who should be my Mate? Should I even have a mate? Some may never get married, but for most of us, over two-thirds of our life will be spent in a relationship with someone. Knowing what to look for, and who to look for, is key. Preparing for marriage is one of the best things a person can do. Two of the biggest reasons many marriages fail are "lack of preparation" and "unrealistic expectations." Marriage can be the second greatest source of joy on earth, or one of the biggest sources of pain.

For the next few years, I wrestled with "Who is my Master?" I also dabbled in different careers looking for my mission. And I was definitely searching for someone to be my mate!

Maybe you don't need a bumper sticker. Maybe you just need some colorful, coated candies to remind you of the three most important questions in life. They won't melt in your hands, but they could change your heart! Much of this book is my attempt to answer those three basic, but immensely important, questions.

I wish I had spent more time thinking about what is most important. For many years, I wasn't even sure what was important, let alone what to look for in life, or a wife!

Then I found a quote that summed it up beautifully:

"The best love is the kind that awakens the soul and makes us reach for more, that plants a fire in our hearts and brings peace to our minds."—Nicholas Sparks, *The Notebook*

And that's what I have in my life and with my wife. I hope you have, too, or at least are looking for it.

CHAPTER 22
ROCKY BALBOA &
THE PINK PANTHER

"*Growing up, when it came to the opposite sex, I was a confirmed agnostic. I believed girls existed; I just had no personal conversion experience.*"—Robert G. Lee

"*I still remember my first kiss! Woooeee! I felt a chill run down my spine... Her Popsicle was melting!*"—Don Lonie

"*Looking for a man? I think men who have a pierced ear are better prepared for marriage. They have experienced pain and bought jewelry.*"—Rita Rudner

"*They're kissing again. Do we have to read the kissing parts?*" —The Grandson, *The Princess Bride*

My future fiancée was quiet. I didn't notice she was there, and she didn't know she would become my wife. She was part of our youth group. My pastor, Bill Neff, was her pastor's son. The young people from two different churches had met and merged. Kids from 7th grade to college now met every Thursday and Sunday night to sing songs like *It Only Takes a Spark to Get a Fire Going* and *If That Isn't Love*. And finding love was a major reason guys went to youth group, at least for this guy! It was one of the three M&M's.

Dawn didn't really stand out. She sat quietly in the corner, her long red hair almost always in a bun, with bangs ending just above those glasses that make your eyes look like a cat. She didn't answer many questions during Bible study, but she took lots of notes.

One day, something happened that changed my view of her. My good friend, Donnie, asked her out. You never notice how pretty someone is until someone else takes her out. It was like a '50s black-and-white movie, where the librarian meets a handsome leading man like Cary Grant. That would be like George Clooney for the younger readers, or sticking with Philly guys… Bradley Cooper.

Somehow, in the movies, two unlikely people end up on a date—a great-looking leading man and the timid, plain librarian type. Events lead them together, and after the date, her glasses come off, the pin holding the hair in a bun comes out, and it slowly falls over her shoulders. The hunk of a leading man gives a look of surprise, then a smile of admiration spreads across his face. She looks at him tentatively, longing in her eyes. Their faces slowly move closer and closer, eyes closed, as their lips gently touch in a tender first kiss. As they pull away, their eyes open to gauge the response and see if there is an invitation for an encore. Upon seeing a smile replacing her fear, he moves in again. But I digress.

Perhaps the greatest version of this type of scene is in the greatest love story on film—*Rocky*! When the bumbling boxer makes his move on Adrian, he's standing in the hallway, muscleman T-shirt on, muscles bulging. Adrian, leaning against the wall, is clearly nervous and uncomfortable. Rocky utters that classic line, "I'm gonna kiss ya. You don't have to kiss me back if you don't want to."

Rocky really is a love story, and to this day, it is the only movie I have ever been to where the entire audience stood up and cheered at the end. And perhaps it helped inspire this skinny stud muffin to look for love in the girl next door.

Because, all of a sudden, I looked at Dawn for the first time with new eyes. Sadly, though, she was "in a relationship." My good friend Donnie had begun to date her. It was amazing how much better she suddenly looked. How did I not see her earlier? Now, I had to wait, and waiting is hard for most people, and for folks like me with ADD, it's worse. But I knew it would be a matter of time before she would be on the dating market again. In those days, Donnie didn't date girls too long. I knew if I waited, she would soon be available. I was right. Quicker than you can say "You've been dumped," Donnie had a new squeeze.

I was ready to sweep her off her feet.

"On the rebound" or not, I moved in and asked Dawn out. I wanted to be the one taking out the hairpin, and... well, you know. So, one night after youth group, I asked her out, and she said, "NO!" I couldn't believe it. Apparently, her broken heart needed some healing, so I waited for two whole weeks and asked again. And she said "NO!" Still, I pursued her for several months, calling her, leaving notes on her windshield, rushing to sit next to her at youth group. Law officers might say I stalked her. At a recent "Sweetheart" banquet, we were asked to list the greatest quality of our spouse. Of all the things she could have listed, like "sense of humor," good dancer, godly man, and a few other things I suggested she put down, she said, "Persistence."

Here's how it happened. It was a steamy summer night when our youth group went to the movies at the TriState Mall in Delaware. (Note to parents—group dating is a great alternative to those dangerous one-on-one dates!) Peter Sellers was starring in *The Pink Panther*. Our group swarmed the box office. When Dawn went to pay for her ticket, I jumped the line, plopped down a ten-dollar bill, and said, "TWO PLEASE!" She smiled

159

as I handed her one of the tickets. A good sign. And when our group entered the theater, we took our seats—together. Can you hear the theme to *Rocky* playing in your mind!

The crowd laughed at Kato's attempts to attack Inspector Clouseau, and roared at classic lines like, "Does your dog bite?" "No." CHOMP! "I thought you said your dog doesn't bite." "It's not my dog." Normally, I'd be in hysterics at such brilliant comedy, but I was distracted. I kept peaking at her hand just inches from mine, wondering what would happen if I tried to hold it. My heart pounded and my mouth was dry as my mind played out a variety of approaches to grasp her fingers. This is much harder than you think. See, for a skinny kid like me, it takes both hands and a lot of effort to get those movie seats to stay down. But I took a deep breath, reached out, and miracles of miracles, she didn't pull away. I took a quick look away from the screen and saw her sitting there with her red hair in a bun and her bangs trimmed just above those glasses. She glanced at me and smiled. She smiled! And if memory serves me correct, there was a definite little squeeze of my hand. Oh, there was no doubt in my mind she was "the one."

We have been holding hands for over thirty-five years now. Dawn has new glasses and is still pretty quiet, at least compared to me. I talk; she listens and giggles… a lot. And most times, she wears her hair down! And I like it that way.

I WISH I KNEW

I wish I knew more about love, dating, and relationships. Love is worth looking for, and worth waiting for. And we often find it in people and places we didn't expect.

"You see, I feel sorrier for you than I do for him, because you will never know the things that love can drive a man to... The ecstasies, the miseries, the broken rules, the desperate chances, the glorious failures, and the glorious victories. All these things you will never know, simply because the word 'love' isn't written into your book!"—Dr. McCoy, *Star Trek*, "The Requiem Methuselah"

"The Eskimos have fifty-two words for snow because it is important to them. There ought to be as many words for love."— Margaret Atwood

CHAPTER 23
MY WIFE—
THE KNOCKOUT

"I hate the waiting room. Because it's called the waiting room, there is no chance of not waiting. It's built, designed, and intended for waiting. Why would they take you right away when they have this room all set up?"—Jerry Seinfeld

A guy in a taxi wanted to speak to the driver, so he leaned forward and tapped him on the shoulder. The driver screamed, jumped up in the air, and yanked the wheel over. The car mounted the curb, demolished a lamppost, and came to a stop inches from a shop window. The startled passenger said, "I didn't mean to frighten you. I just wanted to ask you something." The taxi driver says, "It's not your fault, sir. It's my first day as a cab driver... I've been driving a hearse for the past 25 years."—From the Files of Tommy Moore

When Dawn and I were first married, we used to have pillow fights and try to knock each other off the bed. Our own version of "King of the Bed." Which is kind of strange, when you think about it. One night, I leaned over her to tickle her, and she brought her knees up really fast and caught me in the jaw. Next thing I remember, she was looking over the side of the bed where I lay on the floor, seeing stars. We have been playing "Queen of the Bed" ever since!

Two months later, my wife and I were in separate beds, staring at the ceiling, not speaking to each other. The lighted numerals on the clock said it was three in the morning. Glancing over, I saw tears in her eyes and pain in her face. No, we didn't have a fight—we were in an automobile accident. And now, we were laying side by side on gurneys in the hall of the local hospital. Why the hall? The emergency room was packed with the usual weekend tragedies, most from drunk drivers. I felt a little like Joseph. No room for me... or should I say "us."

Now, some of my funniest thoughts come between three and four in the morning, and this was no exception.

We left church late that night after decorating for our "Fall Youth Event." I would say Halloween party, but I know that I'd lose half my readers. Would it be better if I called it a Harvest Festival? Or tell you we dressed up as *Bible* characters?

Whatever you want to call it, it was in late October. We were driving down Monroe Street, just after the Media Theater let out. Folks rushed to their cars, not always waiting for the traffic lights to change. I don't remember much except headlights, screams, and people gathering around our car, telling me help was on the way. I am forever grateful to the EMTs and firemen who show up in the midst of tragedies no matter what time of day or night.

So, there we lay, side by side, not saying a word, hurting, confused, and scared, when a cry pierced the quiet. Long and loud and clear, I heard my name echoing down the hall. "GOOORRRRDOOOON!"

"Hey, Dawn, I'm right here!"

She slowly turned her head to look for me just three feet away. "Owww, my head hurts. What happened?"

"We were hit."

"Hit by what?"

"A truck."

Then, as if I had just gotten home from work, she said quietly, "Oh." Several minutes passed when the loud cry of "GOOOORRDDOONN!" came again.

"Here I am, Dawn."

She turned her head toward my voice, and said, "OWWW, my head hurts. What happened?"

"We were hit." "Hit by what?" "A truck." This was followed by a pause as she considered the info and then said, "Oh." About two minutes later, it started again. "GOOOORDON!!" Again and again, for over an hour, this same conversation took place. Now, you all know I have ADD issues. Call it shock, call it comedy, call it just plain cruel, but I just can't do the same thing over and over—or resist a chance to try something funny.

So, the next time the cry of "GOOORRRRDOON" echoed down the hall, I said, "Here I am," and she turned and said, "OWWWW, my head hurts. What happened?" I made up a story just to see what kind of reaction I could get from her (and from some of the medical staff who were now listening in).

"Shhhh!" I whispered. "Not so loud. They might hear you."

"Who?" she asked innocently.

"Those people over there are Russian agents. They want us to give them the codes to destroy the world."

She listened, considered my story, and said quietly, "Oh."

It didn't take too long before she called out again. "Dawn, don't move. We've been abducted by aliens, and they are removing body parts." Pause. "Oh." The crowd of nurses and doctors gathered around to see how many new stories I could come up with. From cops thinking we were Bonnie and Clyde to "We are testing mattresses for Serta," no matter how outlandish or outrageous the story, her response was always the same. She stared at the ceiling, considered what I said, and then quietly said, "Oh."

It took months for us to recover. She finished her senior year in college and graduated with honors. She has no memory of the year before the accident. Which was great for me. For a while, every time we passed an expensive restaurant, I asked if she remembered the time we ate there! Eventually she caught on. But this accident was an early wake-up call to treasure every day, for tomorrow isn't promised to any of us.

I WISH I KNEW

I didn't know how powerful and effective humor could be. Here are some thoughts from the original Patch Adams, who taught the world how much a good laugh can help.

Although humor itself is difficult to evaluate, the response to humor—laughter—can be studied quite readily. Research has shown that laughter increases the secretion of the natural chemicals (catecholamines and endorphins) that make people feel peppy and good. It also decreases cortisol secretion and lowers the sedimentation rate, which implies a stimulated immune response. Oxygenation of the blood increases and residual air in the lungs decreases. Heart rate initially speeds up and blood pressure rises; then the arteries relax, causing heart rate and blood pressure to lower. Skin temperature rises as a result of increased peripheral circulation.

Thus, laughter appears to have a positive effect on many

cardiovascular and respiratory problems. In addition, laughter has superb muscle-relaxant qualities. Muscle physiologists have shown that anxiety and muscle relaxation cannot occur at the same time and that the relaxation response after a hearty laugh can last up to forty-five minutes... I have reached the conclusion that humor is vital in healing the problems of individuals, communities and societies. I have been a street clown for thirty years and have tried to make my own life silly—not as that word is currently used, but in terms of its original meaning. "Silly" originally meant good, happy, blessed, fortunate, kind, and cheerful... I emphasize being goofy, so most of the humor is at the expense of the giver.

—From *Gesundheit!* by Patch Adams, M.D.

CHAPTER 24
WHAT CAN YOU GET
FOR A QUARTER?

"People love deals. I was at Sam's Club and saw this old couple in line buying a giant bottle of ketchup. It was like a five-gallon bottle. I laughed as I thought to myself, 'You two will be gone long before that ketchup is.'"—Elayne Boosler

"You used to be able to get a week's worth of candy for a quarter. You can't do that anymore—too many cameras!"—From the Files of Tommy Moore

"Your mama is so fat, if she sat down on a quarter, a booger would come out of Washington's nose."—Paula Poundstone

Oops, I forgot something important. So, let's look back a few months. I proposed, Dawn said yes, and her parents gave us their blessing. Months went by as we planned our perfect day. When the wedding was a few weeks off, Dawn didn't seem her normal self. Sure, she had a lot on her plate: planning our big day while working a forty-hour-a-week job, going to college, and all the stuff she did at her house. But clearly something was bothering her. Her bottom lip quivered the way it does when she's really upset, and she whispered, "My doctor said I might not be able to have children." She had gone to an OB/GYN as part of our premarital preparations.

It was hard to hide our profound disappointment. "This has to be wrong!" I shouted. Denial is often a first response to bad news and tragedy. For us, this was both.

I love kids and planned to have a lot of them. I had dreamed of raising my own football team, or baseball team, or basketball team, or maybe, at the very least, a golf partner. Now we were being told that kids were not going to be a part of that plan. We made a return appointment to confront this doctor. He explained some medical malady that would make conception difficult and birthing near impossible.

That changed everything. Well, not everything. We still got married on a hot, humid day in August of 1979. We remained very involved in leading the youth of our two churches. We attended yearly retreats, like the one that so changed my life, as well as some other church and camp events. There was also growing interest in this funny skinny guy who did some comedy and could share a message that teens and parents could relate to. Those churches kept calling me, filling up the rest of my schedule.

We didn't have cell phones way back then, but most homes now had several phones, along with the one on the wall in the kitchen. That one had a three-foot cord, so there was no privacy. Rich people had the six-foot cord that stretched to the closet, or maybe to the sink. And don't get me started on party lines—there was no party. You had to keep lifting up the receiver and listen to see if you got a dial tone, or if someone else was using the phone.

Still, the world was getting smaller. You could talk to anyone, almost anywhere—something that wasn't true a few years earlier. And sometimes we all need someone to talk to. So, one day, while getting ready to speak at a youth event, an idea came to me. I got some 3x5 index cards, wrote my phone number on them, and Scotch-taped a quarter to each one. "Why a quarter?" the kids ask. Because in our day, we had pay phones. You had to put money in to get a signal, and I wanted to connect with any kid, or every kid, who needed someone to talk to.

Something changed in me when I prayed that prayer in 1975. Not only were my sins forgiven, but I had a new life and a new heart. This heart was not only clean, it cared for people other than myself. I have learned that God will never make a bad thing good, but He can make something good come out of a bad thing. Amazing! He took my empty, lonely, hurting heart and filled it. My new heart had a love for kids who were hurting. God took the worst things in my past and gave me a desire to help others who were going through the same thing.

There were times in my life when I didn't know which way to turn, or who to talk to about life, sex, God, or my future plans and fears. So, here was my chance to help someone else. For a year or so, my wife and I made up these cards any time an invitation to speak came in. We were a newly married couple with good jobs, no kids, and—don't be too impressed—it wasn't a lot of money. Each time I handed out the cards, I said, "If you ever need someone to talk to, or someone to pray with, you can call me."

Corny, right? But how I wished there was someone like that for me during my high-school years, and even as a new husband a few years later. Just a few summers ago, my family was walking down the boardwalk in Ocean City, New Jersey, one of our favorite places. Outside the Wonderland Pier, with all the rides, a young woman called my name! Well, she actually yelled, "HEY! Aren't you that funny preacher guy? Did you speak at my camp in 1985?"

"Yes, that was me!" I said, beaming that someone could recognize me more than twenty-five years later.

As she came closer, she opened her purse and said, "Look at this!" She then pulled out the card with a quarter still taped to it. She said quietly, "I will never forget that you said there was someone out there who cared about me."

When you offer love and hope to a world starving for real love and desperate for hope, people will call. After sharing my story at a few camps and youth events, our first call came. A fourteen-year-old boy from Philadelphia was in a crisis situation and needed help. The next thing you know, he was living with us. His family gave us legal custody while they worked out a few things in a recently blended home. Kids in trouble often know kids in trouble, and soon a second young man moved in. Not long after that, a third.

Without violating any privacy issues or breaking any laws, I'll tell you one had a dad in jail, one hadn't seen or spoken to his dad in years, and one watched his mother try to murder his dad—a woman who would, when the trial was over, spend years in jail.

So, our family was growing. Oh, there's more. We were only married for two years when Dawn's mother Martha died at age forty-six. Two years after that, Dawn's dad, Charlie, had a stroke and moved in with us. Joining Charlie was Dawn's brother, Chuckie. Chuckie had Down syndrome. He had the mind of a four-year-old in a twenty-year-old body. If you ever want to know what God's unconditional love is like, you need to know someone with Down syndrome. They have an extra chromosome, which I think gives them an extra dose of love. Chuckie and Charlie lived with us for the next eighteen years before the Lord called them both home just a few weeks apart.

We now had the three boys, my father-in-law, and my brother-in-law, but it didn't stop there. Whenever one of "our boys" graduated or moved on, another one just seemed to show up. We never advertised, and we had no training in counseling or dealing with addiction or abuse. We just had an open home and open hearts. That's all it took, and folks started coming. For the next twenty-five years, we had a series of visitors and houseguests, many of whom became part of our unusual family.

People ask, "Your website says you have nineteen kids. Is that true, or is that a joke?"

"Noooo!" I respond with a straight face. "Actually, we have twenty-three. We just don't like four of them!"

The truth is we stopped counting at twenty-three, and some were easier to love than others. But, to clarify, it was usually three at a time, plus my father-in-law and brother-in-law. We did not adopt, or do foster care—we just gave folks a place to stay, some time to heal, and get some "life training." Some were teens, some were young adults, a married couple, a few missionaries, add in a couple of exchange students, and there you have it. Usually we had 11-15 folks living with us. Some were in ministry, some were out of ministry, and all needed ministry.

A typical family dinner. It's even more chaotic than it looks.

We are here for a reason, I believe a bit of the reason is to throw little torches out to lead people out of the dark."—Whoopi Goldberg

You don't have to open your home, but I would challenge you to open your eyes and heart. There are a ton of folks in your world who need a friend, or a call, a meal, a hug, or a prayer. Maybe you could open your wallet and sponsor a kid, or pay for a meal. Maybe serve a meal at a soup kitchen, or be a Big Brother or Sister, or...

CHAPTER 25
PROS & CONS

So, this guy goes to prison, his first day he hears a guy call out 32 and everybody laughs! Another guy calls out 64 and everybody laughs!

He says to his cellmate, "What's that about?"

Cellmate says, "We're telling jokes. We've all been here so long, we know them all. We just number them and call out the number."

Guy says, "Can I try?" Cellmate says, "Sure."

Guy says "41." Nobody laughs. He tries again, a bit louder. "41!" and it stayed quiet. He says, "How come nobody laughed?"

Cellmate says, "Well, some guys just can't tell a joke!"

Next day, he tries again. He says, "552." Biggest laugh ever!

He says, "How come they laughed so much this time?"

Cellmate says, "We never heard that one before!"
—From the Files of Tommy Moore

Actual questions from real trials:

"Were you alone or by yourself?"
"Was it you or your brother who was killed?"
"Without saying anything, tell the jury what you did next."
"Was that the same nose you broke as a child?"
"Now, doctor, isn't it true that when a person dies in his sleep, he doesn't know about it until the next morning?"
—From *The Dumb Book* (Reader's Digest Books)

We live near a prison. In fact, if I look right out my back window, I can see it. We used to set our clocks to the noontime whistle. When there is that rare escape, the special whistle blows, a phone chain is set off, and helicopters hover. Most want to get as far away as possible, so we feel pretty safe most of the time.

But there was a time when prisoners were in our house. Really. They didn't break in—we invited them. Actually, the prison called churches in the area. Due to overcrowding, they were looking for folks to allow some off their "residents" to stay in their homes under "house arrest" while they awaited trial. And we volunteered. Why not?

I had read Keith Green's book *No Compromise*. Keith was a child actor turned singer who signed a five-year record deal at the age of twelve. His conversion was dramatic, and so was his life after that. He and his wife, Melody, began helping people in trouble. Wikipedia reports it this way: "They eventually ran out of space (in their home) and, purchased the home next door to their own, and then went on to rent an additional five houses in the same neighborhood. They provided an environment of Christian teaching for a group of young adults, the majority of whom were of college age. Much to the consternation of neighbors, there came to be 75 people living in the Green's homes and traipsing down the suburban streets—including recovering drug addicts and prostitutes, bikers, the homeless, and many single pregnant girls needing shelter and safety. Some were referred to the Greens by other ministries and shelters, but most just crossed their path during their normal life at home and on the road. In 1977, the Greens personal outreach became a non-profit ministry they called Last Days Ministries."

His life inspired me, and his music blesses me, with lines like, "Jesus rose from the dead, and you, you can't even get out of bed" or "My eyes are dry, My faith is old, My heart is hard, My prayers are cold, And I know how I ought to be, Alive to You and dead to me." Keith Green is not the greatest vocalist—more Joe Cocker than Andrea Bocelli—but his lyrics and his passion will pierce your heart.

So, although we were newlyweds, our home was really growing. There was Dawn and me, Charlie (who had a stroke), and Chuckie (Dawn's brother with Down syndrome). Oh, and don't forget to add the three boys from troubled homes. And then, straight from the clink, a couple, around thirty years old, who came to spend time in our home, or I guess "do time" would be more accurate. Oh, wait there's more. During this ten-year period, God showed His sense of humor and proved the doctors wrong by blessing us with five miracle birth children! Four before the doctors told me what was causing it!

For the sake of the story, we will call this couple "John and Lisa." In fact, that's what we did call them. No need to change their names—they weren't innocent. Security was tough; there was an ankle bracelet that beeped if they went further than one hundred feet from the sensor. They could walk about the house and sit on the porch. We set up a bedroom in the basement for them. It started well, as John helped me do some work in my woodshop, and Lisa helped with the kids. They joined us for meals. Lisa tried to convert us to becoming vegetarians. She tried, but failed, God bless her. You know the word "vegetarian" is an old Indian word, right? It's what the Chippewa called a "bad hunter!"

Our court system being backlogged, it took a bit longer than expected for their case to go to trial. Months longer. Lisa was a sweetheart and was intrigued both by Keith Green's story and our willingness to house them. We discussed all kinds of things. Some would even say she was philosophical. To me, she was a free-spirited hippie who wanted to legalize drugs, but she was searching, and one day she prayed with us. The same prayer I prayed back in 1975 at Bible camp. And, well, things began to change, but not all for the good.

John did not seem so excited about her new life and attitude. He was still stuck in this house with us "Jesus Freaks." His anger erupted more than once. He had some bad experience with a pastor or church. That happens a lot. But sometimes we get angry when we don't get what we want, or when something we want gets blocked. That's one of the best things I learned in a counseling class. When we don't get what we want—whether it's a car going slow in front of us when we're in a hurry, or someone gets the promotion we think we deserve, or a spouse or parent or child doesn't do what we want or expect them to do—the dominant emotion is anger. Not all anger is bad, but most is, and anger is a big problem in and out of the church.

After several clear warnings, John's temper exploded again. The consequences had been set in stone, and at my insistence, he was leaving our home. Stupidly, we got in the car. We drove down the highway (doing the speed limit, of course). John apologized, as he always did, and begged me to turn around. It's not easy to administer tough love, but I wasn't budging. I repeatedly refused his request. John then reached over, grabbed the gear shift, threw it into reverse, and then park.

It is hard to describe the sound your engine makes when that happens, but the car does stop… pretty quickly. He grabbed the keys out of the ignition, threw them into the weeds, and took off, running down the highway. (Funny that the word "weed" made it into this story.)

It didn't take long to find my keys. Offering a quick prayer as I inserted the key into the ignition, the car started. One gear still worked, and I cruised home at a solid fifteen miles per hour, where I called the police. It didn't take long to find John, either. Let's just say John's new roommate was not near as pretty as his wife.

Sometime later, he was allowed to return to our home. I hoped he had learned not to mess with me, but I was wrong. It didn't take too long before I heard a lot of yelling in the basement. When I walked down the steps, I saw Lisa sitting on the bed with a bloody lip, and John was now holding my sledge hammer. John wanted out, and apparently, she didn't want to make the big escape with him. She went upstairs with me, and John began destroying the furniture.

Trying to be like Clint Eastwood in Dirty Harry, but guessing I sounded more like Barney Fife, I said, "John, you have one minute to put down the sledge and calm down, or I'm calling the police and you're done here!" He ranted and raved and accused me of not being a good Christian, and how he was being framed, and on and on. *Yeah, this is all my fault, or their fault—never yours*, I thought.

I counted down. "Forty-five seconds, John…" "Thirty

seconds, John..." "Ten seconds, John..." He didn't seem to care, or he thought I was bluffing, as he continued to rage. When I speak on parenting, I tell folks you need the 3 C's: Clear, Consistent Consequences. Convicts and kids both need to know where the lines are and what will happen when those lines are crossed. It drives me nuts to hear parents threaten and threaten their kids, and then watch the kids defy them. And then it gets worse, as parents draw a new line in the sand, with no consequences. AAAAUUGH!!

Josh McDowell has a great quote that balances out this principle of the Three C's. It's the Three R's: "Rules without Relationship lead to Rebellion." Our children need to know what the boundaries are, and what the consequences will be if they are crossed. But just as important, children need to know that "the boundaries, curfews, and rules" are there because we love them and want what is best for them. "Because I love you is so much more powerful than BECAUSE I SAID SO!" It's one of the most important things I ever learned. But I digress (again!).

Well, John's time was up. Not his sentencing, but my generous grace period during his meltdown. There wasn't much left in the basement he could break. So, I walked up the steps and called the state police. Their barracks are just a few minutes from our home. Soon this would be all over, right? Wrong! There was a snowstorm in Philly that winter—a really big snowstorm. Over thirty inches of snow fell. I could barely see out the bay window in the living room as I searched for the police car to pull up my long driveway. Five… ten… fifteen minutes went by. The good news was that John was not going to escape in this storm.

I peered out the window for the next forty-five minutes, praying that John would stay in the basement. And what to my wondering eyes should appear? Not a man in a red suit, but the army in full gear! Apparently, cop cars are not equipped for that kind of snow, so, they called in the National Guard. A big green truck with giant wheels and green canvas, just like in the movies. Men in camouflage with rifles surrounded my house. Okay, my wife said it was two men in a Humvee, plus the two state troopers, but I remember at least five trucks and twenty men. My wife put on some more hot cocoa. She is like that. Such a servant.

The officers came in, stamping the snow off their feet, obviously not thrilled to be called out in this weather. I explained the situation while John was summoned from the basement. John was 6'5" and solid and scary, and what he did next was so weird. Right there, in front of the men in uniform, he fell to his knees and started kissing my hand like he wanted a papal pardon. Over and over he kissed my hand and begged me for mercy. I had seen this act before and wasn't budging. I wanted him, in the words of Harry Kalas, the famed Phillies baseball broadcaster…. "OUTTA HERE!"

The police asked Lisa if she wanted to press charges. John

looked up with puppy-dog eyes and expressed his sorrow, and from his knees promised it would never ever happen again, reaching out to hold her hand. She had seen this before, as well, and said through swollen lips that she wanted him gone. Like Lou Ferrigno in *The Incredible Hulk*, John changed instantly. One moment he was on his knees, the next on his feet yelling and screaming and threatening us all. As the police cuffed him, John yelled, "You better check her identity. Her real name is not Lisa." Lisa's jaw dropped, and her face turned as white as the snow outside.

Not to be outdone, she sneered and said, "You men need to check his background because he's wanted by the police overseas!" I kid you not. They started diming on each other. We learned they were not the sweet young couple we once thought.

Who were they? We still aren't sure because we never saw them again. When the parole officer came to pick up the computer for the ankle bracelets, he apologized and said they should never have been in the program. Sorry! Sorry?? So, we were misinformed and a bit naive. Something good came out of it, though. While they were here, we invented a game. When someone would visit, we lined up everyone in the living room and asked our guests to guess "Which one is the convict?" You know, if you cover up that ankle bracelet, it's hard to tell!

It's a joke, but a joke with a point. When I ask folks, "Who do you think God loves more—the pastor or the prisoner?", they always say the pastor. But when I ask the audience, "In God's eyes, what is the difference between a pastor and a prisoner?" most shrug their shoulders. The answer, of course, is the prisoner got caught! Pastors never laugh at that joke, but the truth is, in God's eyes, there is no difference. "We have all sinned and fallen short of the glory of God," says Saint Paul in Romans 3:23. And we all need forgiveness, whether for things said and done in anger, or out of stubbornness, stupidity, or pride.

The key is whether we are on the run from God, or on the run to God. No matter how far we've gone, it's always just one step back to God.

I WISH I KNEW

"I wish I knew that not everything we did would be easy and turn out great. But I have learned that even in what seemed like failure, it is worth trying to make a difference."—Mother Theresa

Mother Theresa also sums it up well in this poem, *Do It Anyway*, written on the wall of her home for children:

People are often unreasonable, illogical and self-centered;
Forgive them anyway.

If you are kind, people may accuse you of selfish, ulterior motives;
Be kind anyway.

If you are successful, you will win some false friends and some true enemies;
Succeed anyway.

If you are honest and frank, people may cheat you;
Be honest and frank anyway.

What you spend years building, someone could destroy overnight;
Build anyway.

If you find serenity and happiness, they may be jealous;
Be happy anyway.

The good you do today, people will often forget tomorrow;
Do good anyway.

Give the world the best you have, and it may never be enough;
Give the world the best you've got anyway.

You see, in the final analysis, it is between you and your God;
It was never between you and them anyway.

CHAPTER 26
IS THAT YOU, GOD?

Quotes from the movie *Oh, God!* starring John Denver as Jerry and George Burns as God.

Jerry Landers: People are always praying to you. Do you listen?
God: I can't help hearing. I don't always listen.

Court Clerk: Do you swear to tell the truth, the whole truth, and nothing but the truth?
God: So help Me, Me.
Judge Baker: So help you, You?

God: The last miracle I did was the 1969 Mets. Before that, I think you have to go back to the Red Sea.

God: The reason I put everyone here naked... I wasn't trying to be cute. It's just that with clothes, right away there's pockets, and pockets, you gotta put something in 'em.

Jerry Landers: You know, I'm... I'm liable to lose my job.
God: Lose a job, save a world. Not a bad deal.

It's not so hard to picture George Burns as God. Not when you grow up with a TV show called *My Mother the Car*! It starred Jerry Van Dyke, the brother of Dick Van Dyke. The premise of this 1965 show is that the mother of attorney David Crabtree dies and is reincarnated as a classic car—a 1928 Porter to be precise. And she talks through the radio, but only her son can hear her. *TV Guide* rated it the second worst show in television history. In 1982, there was another car named KITT that talked to David Hasselhoff in a show called *Knight Rider*. A little more trivia—in 1989, Jerry Van Dyke became famous on the hit show *Coach*, but back in 1964, he turned down a role in a series that he didn't think would be a hit. He chose *My Mother the Car* over the starring role on *Gilligan's Island*. And the rest is history!

Stanger things have happened, like the time my truck talked to me. Really. The voice was low and slow, yet clear. Not real loud, but there was no mistaking it. As I sat at the red light, I quickly looked around me. I didn't see anyone or anything, but I definitely heard a voice. Turning off the radio, I could still hear it. There were no other cars at the intersection; no one else riding with me. "Is that you, God?" I had been praying to hear God's voice for some time, but in my little red truck... at a stoplight? Yet, the voice clearly uttered a few lines from the *Bible*.

The light turned green and as I pulled out, the voice got quiet. Stopping at the next red light, I heard it again! This happened four times as I drove along. Each time I stopped, the voice began, always with some reference to a *Bible* passage.

Now, I know that I serve a God who sees and who hears me when I call. A God who even collects my tears in a bottle. But this God who speaks is scary. I have heard too many people who claimed that GOD TOLD ME TO... (you can complete the sentence), even when what they are told is clearly contrary to God's written Word. I am skeptical. I admit it. Like, if God told me to leave my wife and marry Taylor Swift. I can say He said it, but it's clearly against His written Word, and I am not sure Taylor and I are compatible.

But as I read the *Bible*, it's clear that God does, in fact, speak. Yes, through His Word, and never ever ever ever contrary to it. The *Bible* is filled with stories of when he spoke through dreams, impressions, angels, other people, and circumstances. Most people who claim to hear God speak say it is clear, but not really an audible voice. It's similar to hearing a human voice, but not quite the same. A loud thought, perhaps?

I want to learn. I don't want to miss God's best. And communication is a major key in any relationship. When most people pray, they ask God for stuff. Rarely do we see prayer as a two-sided conversation. Learning to spend a few minutes each day just listening—not asking God for anything, or rambling on and on with my concerns and questions. This has been a big change for me. The Holy Spirit does lead, prompt, convict, illuminate, and bring verses to mind to give insight. One fundamental pastor I love argued with me, however, claiming strongly "that GOD DOES NOT SPEAK anymore. He only speaks through His Word." After our discussion, I asked what he was preaching on this week, and he excitedly told me how he prayed for the right message, and as he studied, he just happened to come across a passage that just lit his spiritual fire, allowing him to address a need in the congregation. Hmmm, sounded like God communicated with him.

So, who was speaking in my truck?

When I got home and reached over to take out my toolbox, I saw my cassette player under the driver's seat. When I stopped at a red light, apparently it slid forward and a wire under the seat pressed the "play button" down, just enough to make it play. When the light turned green and I pulled out, it slid back a few inches and went off. It was playing a sermon, but with weak batteries, the voice was hauntingly slow but clear. And scary! And get this, it was a sermon by the guy who said that God doesn't speak anymore! Is that wild or what?

I WISH I KNEW

I wish I knew earlier that God speaks today. If God were to

189

speak to you today? What do you think He would say? I've got some ideas. Twenty years ago, I imagined God would say, "Hey, you, knock that off!" "STOP THAT!" or "Don't make me come down there!" Now, I think it would be more "I love you!" "Let Me help you! I want what is best for you!" "Why are you running from Me?" His Word is still the best way to hear God's heart, but I have learned that he speaks in many other ways.

"We have mouths that close and ears that don't. That ought to teach us something!" says Rick Warren. Neale Donald Watson adds, "God is speaking to all of us, all the time. The question is not to whom does God talk? The question is, 'Who is listening?'"

"Our failure to hear His voice when we want to is due to the fact that we do not in general want to hear it, that we want it only when we think we need it."—Dallas Willard, *Hearing God: Developing a Conversational Relationship with God*

FIVE TESTS ON HOW TO KNOW IF THIS IS GOD

- IT AGREES WITH SCRIPTURE, and never contradicts a clear command!
- God usually repeats things.
- It often comes as an idea or thought during a time of prayer.
- The desire grows stronger with time.
- There is usually an element of risk and faith involved.

CHAPTER 27
BACK TO THE FUTURE

Marty McFly: Calvin? Why do you keep calling me Calvin?
Lorraine Barnes: Well, that's your name, isn't it? It's written all
over your underwear.
—From *Back to the Future*

"My wife says camping is 'a tradition' in her family. So... wasn't
camping a tradition in everyone's family before we came up
with... the HOUSE?"
—Jim Gaffigan

Have I mentioned that I hate camping? What could be worse than camping with little kids on a hot summer day? How about camping with 70,000 kids on the side of a mountain on a hot summer day? It's called CREATION, a music festival on a farm in central PA. A Christian Woodstock, of sorts, where a multitude reminiscent of the book of Exodus gather to hear some of the best speakers and Christian music in the country. I was a youth pastor, then, and not a very good one. I tried to share my passion for Jesus, stirred by singers like Keith Green and Carmen, but this new generation just didn't seem to connect to me, or to Jesus. Our youth group was so small, we couldn't play *Duck, Duck, Goose*. But wanting to expose my "teens" to the best Christianity has to offer, my three teens joined me on this three-hour trip to the mountains. A three-hour tour—I should have known disaster was ahead.

I was depressed and ready to quit the ministry. I felt like a failure. I heard famous speakers and thought, *I'm a better speaker than them. I am funnier than them. How do they get to speak on that big stage when I can't get three kids to sit still and listen?* After the main speakers, there were workshops in the woods. One, titled "Hearing God's Voice!" caught my attention. So, I followed several hundred, maybe several thousand, folks up the path to Area 5 to hear a young preacher named Francis Anfuso teach us "How God Speaks".

After some basic instructions, Francis said it was easier to show folks than tell them how to do it. He asked for anyone who needed prayer or wanted to hear a "word from God" to come forward. And about fifty people quickly went forward and formed a line. Part of the team with Francis began singing. It was strange because they didn't sing the same song. Some sang a song or two I recognized, others sang a prayer, and

192

some just sang out a note or two like Motown back-up singers. And it was beautiful. Someone seeing my puzzled look said this was "singing in the Spirit."

I got as close as I could to where they were praying, and then leaned in to hear better. For us old folks, it was like the old E.F. HUTTON commercial. One or two folks positioned themselves behind the person in front of the preacher. I learned that this was in case they fell. And a lot of them did. Still not sure what to make of all that. The people who wanted prayer weren't interviewed, or asked what they wanted prayer for. The pastor and his team worshipped quietly, trusting that God would lead them in what to say to each person.

After several moments, Francis would say something like, "God wants you to know He loves you!" or "God has a plan for you!" There were quotes of some familiar verses, but nothing too freaky. In fact, it was pretty cool to see folks respond to some basic *Bible* truths. Some were overwhelmed with emotion; some broke in tears. After praying for a dozen or so folks, music started blaring from down in the valley where the band was warming up. Francis said, "I'm sorry, folks. I'm having trouble hearing. Come back tomorrow, and we'll do this again and answer any questions."

As I grabbed my beach chair and backpack, I heard Francis yell, "You, don't go anywhere—God has a word for you!" I looked around and realized he was pointing at me. ME! Out of all the folks there, He had "a word" for me! I walked toward

Francis and was soon surrounded by folks laying hands on my shoulders. I had a little tape recorder in my pocket to record jokes or funny thoughts when they come to me. I flipped the switch to ON. We stood close, our noses almost touching. I noticed he had a breath mint. "Note to self. If getting close to folks to talk about the Lord, a breath mint is a good idea. How many folks miss eternal blessings because of bad breath?"

"You are hurting right now," he said softly. *DUH!!* I thought, not impressed by this guy's prophetic insights. I had been crying and was obviously depressed. Terrible thoughts filled my mind. Thoughts like, *God couldn't use you. God doesn't love you. You aren't good enough.* It would take years before I learned how to stop those thoughts. But in that moment, Francis continued, "You have a real heart for young people!" *DOUBLE DUH!! Of course I care about youth. I'm a thirtysomething man at a youth conference, you idiot!* My mind often did this flip-flop from condemning myself to severe sarcasm making fun of everyone and everything.

I still wasn't impressed. "You're jealous of the folks on the stage." (Now, how did he know that?) Then he said (and I have the tape and have written this out in my journal), "Someday you are going to speak to thousands."

Wow, I thought, getting excited, no longer doubting that this was GOD. Then he said, "No," and my immediate reaction was, *Rats! I knew it was too good to be true.* "No, you aren't going to speak to thousands, but tens of thousands."

Is this a joke? I thought, but smiled broadly at the thought that someday I could do what these guys do. He stared at me for a moment or two, then said, "NO!" his face grimacing like he was trying to figure out a math problem. He started choking, for real, saying between gasps, "Yuk! I swallowed a bug!" You can hear it on tape as he choked some more. He then prayed a bit more quietly and looked me in the eyes. "Someday, you are going to speak to hundreds of thousands, and your ministry will go around the world."

Okay, now I knew this guy was nuts. He and the others seemed very excited and offered me some words of encouragement, basically saying, "Don't give up. God has a plan for you!"

Those are words that most of us need to hear at one time or another. For me, it was just what I wanted to hear. I listened to my little tape recorder over and over. When I got home, I wrote it in my journal.

Over the next year, the youth group grew, and I got to preach occasionally. But the biggest crowd was maybe ninety folks. And for the next ten years, not much changed. The dream died. Was that really a word from God?

Early on in my training, my pastor, Don Britton, challenged me to start journaling. Once a week, sometimes once a month, I jot down a few thoughts. What I have read or heard that inspired me. A key verse or two. What is going on in our home, or church. Many times, it is some terrible news, and I write out a verse or a prayer. A big part of what I write is what I'm worried about— the car breaking down, the health of a friend, the future of my kids, and where will the money come from for a thousand different things. Now, I have thirty years' worth of stories on how we got through some difficult times.

This was the first time someone prayed over me! A prayer for my future. A future that, to me, didn't look too bright. The rest of this book will highlight how that prophetic prayer was answered, but for you, maybe it's time to write down where you are, what you're facing, and what you're afraid of. Date it. And, in a few weeks or months, you will be amazed how encouraging it will be.

CHAPTER 28
THE BLESSINGS OF BANKRUPTCY

"Someone stole my wife's credit card, but I didn't report it. The thief spends less than my wife!"—Henny Youngman

"Has your neighbor changed since winning the lottery? I don't know, he doesn't talk to me anymore!"—Gene Perret

"Mr. Rockefeller, how much money would it take to make you happy? His answer? "Just a little bit more."

Did you ever dream that Ed McMahon would knock on your door with a team of guys holding a six-foot check for a million dollars? Cameras would record your reaction. Do you know what you would do if you hit the winning ticket and won a million dollars? Recently, some of my co-workers were discussing that very thing during lunch. Buying homes, fancy cars, going on cruises, telling your boss to take this job and… (well, you know!) Some even said they would use part of the money to help their favorite charity.

Did you know that many people who win the lottery said it was the worst thing to ever happen to them? Some lost friends who wanted to mooch. Family members show up wanting to share the blessing. People with life-threatening diseases show up at your door asking for money to get medicine. Marriages end over what to do with the money, and some winners have even taken their lives. But coming into sudden wealth was not my problem—losing money was.

After being laid off from Gulf Oil, I sold my stock—a year later, that stock went on to double in a takeover attempt by T. Boone Pickens. After my father-in-law died, I invested our small inheritance in five dotcom stocks for each of our birth children to pay for their college education. This was right before the bubble burst, and what was left would barely cover a notebook and a pencil.

If there is something I know less about than investing, it is how to run a business. Inspired by my father being in a wheelchair, I started a business where I could put my carpentry skills to good use: Therapeutic Construction and Design, Inc. "Specializing in the design and manufacture of custom furniture for those with physical disabilities." Simply put, we built things for folks in wheelchairs. We even had a patent pending on a chair! Somehow, after several years of hard work and growth, we ran out of money. I blamed my business partner; he blamed me. But we owed tens of thousands of dollars to suppliers. Money we did not have. For legal reasons, I won't go into detail, but I was devastated.

There are few worse feelings in life than having your credit card declined at a store. Or having collection agencies calling you nightly to remind you of your balance and asking, oh, so politely, "How much would you like to take off that balance today?" After a few weeks, the calls were not so nice. Feeling like a failure as a businessman is bad enough, but to not be able to provide for your family is horrible. Trips to McDonald's are out, buying clothes that fit the kids as they grow is put off, and trips to the dentist and other non-essentials are postponed.

It was then, in 1987, that I called Larry Burkette. He had a daily radio show called *Money Matters*. People would call in, ask a question, and Larry would offer advice based on principles in the *Bible*. Some would ask about how much life insurance they should have. Others would ask about investing in gold, or stocks. Many would ask about tithing, particularly on an inheritance, or tax return. But my question was different.

Holding the phone to my ear, I heard the voice of Steve Moore, the announcer, say, "Our next caller is Gordon from Philadelphia, listening to WVCH radio. Gordon, how can we help you?" I got right to the point. "I'm thirty-two years old, I have a wife, two kids, we've taken in a few boys off the street, we have another baby on the way, and I just lost my life savings. My business partner is gone. Oh, and I believe the Lord is calling me into the ministry. What should I do?"

Many friends, businessmen—even other Christians—told me to just declare bankruptcy and start over. Larry did not. He asked me whose name was on the corporation. Mine. Who, then, is responsible to pay off the debt? I didn't like where this was going. "Legally, you could declare bankruptcy, but Biblically, you have a responsibility to do all you can do to pay off your debts." I tried to explain that it wasn't my fault. I didn't lose, or take the money. Nothing I shared seemed to steer him away from being obedient to the *Bible*.

We prayed. We fasted. Well, I'm not sure you call it fasting when you can't afford food, but we sought the Lord and knew deep inside we had to "bite the bullet" and pay off the debt. It took thirteen years of working two jobs, but we did everything we could to pay everyone back. In addition to my already growing and large family, my wife did taxes on the side and babysat for our neighbors. For several years, she watched two adorable redheads that folks thought were ours. Then, new neighbors moved in and needed someone to watch their five-year-old triplets, plus a baby and two older children, which Dawn did for several more years.

We skimped and saved, and God was faithful! It was humbling not to be able to provide stuff, or go places most families did. It is still one of my biggest regrets. We did have fun, though, learned to do a lot with very little. And we saw some amazing things. Bags of clothes and food would be in our garage almost weekly. We would come home from church and find several brown paper bags of food and boxes with some really nice used clothing, along with stuff I assumed we were to use to clean the basement floor. (Okay, that may sound too sarcastic because people meant well, but some stuff people give to folks in ministry is well, to put it bluntly, junk. I appreciate the effort, but what are you supposed to do with used teabags??? I mean, really!)

Oh, that thing about becoming a pastor? Larry said, "If God called you, He will provide. And the Lord most often works through the local church, so tell your pastor and your church your dreams and watch what God does!" I didn't want to tell Larry how stupid that plan was. Our church only had about fifty folks, and our dear pastor was part-time, driving a bulldozer to help pay his bills. I cut the grass there for years and didn't get paid because they had no money, but my mom thought it would be good for me. So, what did I do? After stewing, wrestling with his advice, and praying, I listened to Larry, who told me to listen to God.

That next Sunday, on a hot summer day in our un-air-conditioned sanctuary, I stood up in our "testimony time" and told folks I felt the Lord calling me into ministry. I wanted to go to Bible school, and they graciously prayed for me. I applied to the Institute of Biblical Studies, a one-year "through the Bible program" overseen by The Friends of Israel Ministry in Deptford, New Jersey. I had less than a month before school started.

Not only did I get accepted, but I was awarded a full scholarship. And my pastor called and said someone in the church offered to pay our mortgage for a year. I could fill another whole book on the thousands of answered prayers and the needs that were met, none of which would have happened if I hadn't lost everything. Winning the lottery sounds good, but watching the Lord, Jehovah Jireh, meet your needs, open doors, and restore blessings is the best.

Postscript. For a year, I wondered who would be so kind as to pay my mortgage. In a church that small, I knew we didn't have any really wealthy people. It was a mystery, until one day, it was our family's turn to clean the church. My kids vacuumed the rugs, and my wife cleaned the bathrooms. While, I was dumping the trash in the pastor's office, I saw a check on the desk made out to my Bible school. I couldn't believe the name. Someone I would have never expected, was making it possible for me to follow my dream and fulfill my calling. May their reward be great in Heaven.

Who God uses and who God chooses is still amazing. Just one more person in a long line of folks who helped me get to where I am today. All I can do is be amazed.

I WISH I KNEW

I wish I knew that sometimes we have to take a step of faith before we see an answer. What is holding you back, keeping you from making a call or filling out an application? Don't let a lack hold you back!

"God's work done God's way will never lack God's supply!"
—Hudson Taylor

CHAPTER 29
A HAIRY SITUATION

"What did Don King say when he went to the barber? Can you give me something that makes me look like I am falling down an elevator shaft?"—Kathleen Madigan

"How long does it take to do your hair? I don't know—I'm never there!"—Dolly Parton

"Actually, I comb my hair quite often. I just use an electric toothbrush!"—Phyllis Diller

"Of course it's real hair. It just isn't mine!"—John Wayne

Missed it by a hair! That means it's close, right? How big is a single strand of hair? I looked it up. Europeans consider hair with a diameter of 0.04 to 0.06 mm as thin, hair with a diameter between 0.06 and 0.08 mm as normal, and hair with a diameter between 0.08 and 0.1 mm as thick. Compared to European hair, Asian hair is significantly thicker. The average diameter of Asian hair is 0.08 to 0.12 mm. Bigger, but still tiny. Each strand of hair on the human body is at its own stage of development. Once the cycle is complete, it restarts, and a new strand of hair begins to form. The rate or speed of hair growth is about 1.25 centimeters (0.5 inches), per month. That's about fifteen centimeters, or six inches, per year.

One hair, even a foot in length, is hard to see. Together, a lot of hairs can be beautiful. My wife has long, wavy red hair, as do two of my daughters. The other one has long, blond hair. They comb it, braid it, tease it, curl it, style it, and it looks nice. But where it is not pretty is on my clothes, in my food, and worst of all, in my bathtub. I regularly have to remove a rat's nest from the drain.

Individually, a thin strand is next to nothing. Joined together and multiplied by a thousand (with a little added shampoo residue) and it forms a perfect plug. There are blockages in life, too. Things we do, or attitudes we have, that hinder our growth and level of intimacy. These little offenses build up like the hairs in the tub, or dust on my television screen. I regularly need to clean the drain and wipe the dust off the flatscreen TV. The same is true for my heart and mind. In Psalm 66:18, David called out, "Search me, O, God, and know my heart!"

My youth pastor growing up was Jim Anderton. The guy

could play a guitar, and sing. He reminds me a lot of Keith Green. A favorite lyric—a prayer really—is "Create in me a clean heart, and renew a right spirit with in me!" Jim gave us a sheet taken from the writings of Charles Finney titled *Break Up the Fallow Ground*. It is a series of questions that cause us to reflect on our life and examine our heart. (See Appendix for a list of some of these questions.)

So, there I was, sitting in my extra tall man's La-Z-Boy recliner. In thirty-five years of marriage, there have only been two recliners in our home—both La-Z-Boys. I love that chair. I read, relax, and reflect in it. One quiet Sunday afternoon, I was just getting comfortable in my chair. Now, don't let that fool you. Relaxing for me is sitting and trying to slow my thoughts down to a thousand a minute. Listening to Robin Williams in *Aladdin* rattle off one unscripted line after another may give some insight into the mind of a hyperactive person like me.

It was an exciting time. School started tomorrow. Bible school. A new season in my life was about to begin. I was about to pray the third most important prayer of my life.

Sometimes I think prayers, and sometimes I say them out loud. This one was important enough to speak out loud. I wanted Him to hear me. "Father in Heaven," I prayed, "You have been so good to me. Thanks for this new home, thanks for the kids, thanks for the way You opened doors for me to go to school." Sometimes praise just flows from a heart filled with gratitude. But my heart wasn't filled to the brim. Other stuff crept in.

"Lord, if there is anything in my life that I need to confess, any wrong that needs to be made right, anyone I need to apologize to or forgive, just let me know. I want to have a clean heart, and be as close to You as I can." This is such a good prayer for all of us.

The amen had not escaped my lips when the name of my former business partner immediately came to mind, and anger filled my soul. "Anybody but him, Lord!" Pretty sure that was said out loud, too. I don't know if you've ever argued with God, but there have been more than a few times when the Spirit is clearly leading, prompting, revealing something to me, and I resisted, argued, or ignored the thought. And the feeling that follows is horrible. If there is anything in life that feels worse than being betrayed, lied to, or taken advantage of, it is what I feel when I say no to GOD. It's like when I say something without thinking and upset my wife, and then disappoint my dad, and then don't get invited to that great party all rolled into one. I know that feeling all too well, because as I sense the leading of the Spirit, I learned the distraught feeling and distress that comes when you choose to say no to that leading.

So, I wrestled with the Lord, struggling against the idea of calling the guy I felt, caused me such pain, such loss. This argument went on for some time. Then, the phone rang.

I hadn't spoken to my old business partner in years, but at

that moment, the Lord arranged for him to call me. He was back in town on a side job and wanted to borrow some of my tools. *Are you kidding me? You took almost everything I had, and now you want more?* After a deep breath, I thought of ways to gloat and rub it in, add about thousand insults and putdowns, and then end my diatribe with a loud and clear, "There is no way on God's green earth I am lending you some tools!" Sorry if that seems too harsh, but I can get riled up.

But I didn't say what I was thinking. In a moment, I thought of how blessed my life was, and reviewed, in my hyper mind, all the Lord had done for me in the last ten years. We live in a huge new house we cannot afford, with kids we were told we couldn't have, with a beautiful wife, and I was about to go to school on a full scholarship. I could have said all that. I could have rubbed it in. But I didn't. I invited him over.

It was awkward at first, but we talked. I asked forgiveness for my attitude, and for some things I said to undermine his efforts to get his life back on track. With tears in his eyes, he offered to pay back what he could, when he could. And I lent him some equipment so he could make a little money. Our relationship was still shaky, but it was a start, and my heart was clean.

So now, when I see those long red hairs in my car, in a sandwich, or in a tub, I try to smile and think how blessed I am, and then offer a little prayer to keep my heart clean.

I WISH I KNEW

I wish I knew how much staying angry hurt me. Someone said, "Staying angry is like drinking poison and expecting the other person to die." After years in prison, Nelson Mandela said, "Forgiveness liberates the soul. It removes fear. That is why it is a powerful weapon. When a deep injury is done to us, we never heal until we forgive. As I walked out of the prison door that would lead to my freedom, I knew if I didn't leave my bitterness and hatred behind, I'd still be in prison."

So, what about you? Is there someone who, if you see them or hear their name, makes you cringe inside? It is time to set yourself free. The first step is to choose to forgive. Do it today.

"Son, you may have to declare your forgiveness a hundred times the first day, and the second. But the third day will be less, and each day thereafter, until one day you will realize that you have forgiven completely. And then one day, you will pray for his wholeness and give him over to me so that my love will burn from his life every visage of corruption. As incomprehensible as it sounds at this moment, you may well know this man in a different context one day."—Wm. Paul Young, *The Shack*

CHAPTER 30
THE BROOMALL BOMBER

"They used to call me the Rembrandt of Boxing because I spent so much time on the canvas! I would have won more fights, but the referee kept stepping on my hands."—Bob Hope

"I was what you would call a colorful fighter—mostly black and blue, and a touch of red. I was on my back so often, they used to sell advertising space on the bottom of my shoes! I asked my trainer once, "Should I keep swinging at him?" He said, "Sure, the draft might give him pneumonia!"—Milton Berle

It was the first Thursday in May, which meant we were going to the Media Courthouse for the National Day of Prayer. I parked my truck next to Augie's Hot Dog Stand to unload my sound system. We took the kids out of school to join us for what I believe is one of the most important days of the year.

They were a small part of the hundreds of thousands of people praying for our country. And afterward, they would get a treat from Augie's stand.

August Pantellas was a champion boxer with a record of 28 wins, 6 losses. Though he only stood 5'6" and weighed a mere 130 pounds, his hands were weapons. Just ask the twenty guys he knocked out. His punches were so powerful they called Augie "The Broomall Bomber". How appropriate that name would be by the end of the day.

When Billy Graham came to Philadelphia, I joined dozens of good pastors to lay the groundwork, get trained, and pray. We were taught that when one person prays, it's like shooting a hole into a blanket of darkness over the city, allowing light to peak in. When two people pray, more holes and bigger holes follow. If a group prays and fasts for their city, it's like a bazooka blasting holes through the darkness. Light pours in, and the momentum shifts toward revival.

It was the late '80s when the parishioners from our little church joined hundreds of thousands to pray for our nation on the National Day of Prayer. We invited pastors to bring their flocks to the front steps of the Media Courthouse. Following the lead of my pastor, Pastor Don Britton, I coordinated the gatherings for a few years, and remarkably, they continue to this day. Starting at noon, an hour is spent reading God's Word and praying. Usually, we have a dozen pastors who read, offer a brief comment, and then pray. (Well, the comments are

Me with "The Broomall Bomber", Augie Pantellas. He looks like the athlete I'm trying to be on the cover.

supposed to be brief, but you know pastors. That verse "a day is like a thousand years" is how some sermons feel.) Sometimes, it's a prayer of praise, sometimes a time of confession, sometimes requests are focused on the needs of our country. The hour flies by, and in the end, we break into small groups so everyone has a chance to participate. It is a yearly highlight.

I am moved by everyone who shows up, from the old folks who need help getting their walkers across the grass, to the young moms with babies in strollers. We have been heckled a few times in twenty-five years, but nothing compared to what Stephen went through in Acts 6. At the end, folks are quick to help out by folding chairs, taking apart the sound system, removing the banner, and taking things to my truck. One year, almost two decades ago, one of my boys was with me, packing up the equipment as folks brought it over. Many hands made quick work, and in a few minutes, we headed home.

We were only a few blocks away when several large trucks roared past us going the other way. Large letters spelled out BOMB SQUAD. Marc and I watched them race down the road, wondering what could have happened in our little town. Truth be told, I didn't even know we had a bomb squad. It was when we got home and unloaded the truck that I noticed my briefcase was missing. (Don't get ahead of me! Sometimes I don't put two and two together.) With all the folks helping me pack up and load, my briefcase didn't make it home.

So, back to the courthouse I went. It had only been an hour or so since our event. After finding a coveted parking space, I jogged to the spot where we held our meeting. We looked around the flagpole. Nothing. We went near the giant oak tree where my stuff was stacked, then packed. Nothing. Augie was still there, though, and the lunch crowd was pretty thin. "Hey, Augie, did you happen to see or hear of anyone finding a briefcase?" Okay, a briefcase at a courthouse is as common as a tube top at a NASCAR race.

"Oh, that was yours?" he said with a laugh. He knows I'm

funny, and he has a great laugh, but I didn't get the joke. "You better go inside."

So, up the marble steps and through the giant doors I went. Inside stood several men in uniform, next to the X-ray machine that they make you put your keys and phone through before you can go to a courtroom. "Did someone find a briefcase?" I asked the armed guard innocently.

Rather than talk to me, he spoke into a walkie talkie, and quicker than you can say, "NCIS", several uniformed escorts invited me to follow them. People stared and glared at me as we walked through the long, arched hallways and out the door. Fortunately, the police station was only a few blocks away.

During the walk, they explained to me that someone spotted the briefcase and contacted the bomb squad, who then evacuated the courthouse. Once inside, the police captain took over, explaining the cost of calling in the bomb squad, evacuating the building, delaying trials, and such. Let's do the math, shall we? The cost of lawyer fees at $250 an hour, multiplied by about one hundred lawyers... and apparently, the bomb squad is a tad more expensive than your average limo ride. So, the total bill was more than my cars were worth.

I waited in a little room behind a big window, where there was a lot of whispering. The captain came in with the same look my mom gave me when the principal would call and tell her I did something wrong. You know that look that is a combination of disappointment and disgust. He handed me a piece of paper, showing me the costs involved. Let's just say it was more than I make in a decade. "SIGN THE PAPER!" It wasn't a question. I tried to play it cool, like Matt Damon in *The Bourne Identity* sneaking though customs, staring at the cameras. (I have a sermon titled "The Born (Again) Identity", but I digress.) My voice cracked as I asked what I was signing, as though I would stand up to some torture before caving in. "This is to release you from charges, and to release us for the damage done to your briefcase."

Damage to my briefcase?

Apparently, when X-rayed, my new iPod and earphone wires look a lot like a bomb with a timing device, so, they blew it up. My *Bible* was now edited, my cough drops dissolved, my little bottle of Old Spice that I kept inside to spruce up on sweaty days shattered. This was all easily visible in the cardboard box they handed me, filled with pieces of said briefcase. Still, I realized as I left that day, the greater damage was not to my briefcase, but to the kingdom of darkness. If one can put a thousand to flight, and two could put 10,000, imagine what happens when a nation humbles itself and prays. Prayer is the BOMB that tears down strongholds.

Oh, there was more good news. Augie apparently did very well that day, selling a record amount of hot dogs, as folks waited outside, unable to go back in the courthouse.

People at Augie's Hot Dog Stand on a slightly slower day.

I WISH I KNEW

"I fear the prayers of John Knox more than all the armies of England!"—Mary, Queen of Scots

I wish I knew earlier what happens when we pray, and how to pray. There is so much more to prayer then asking for things. The acronym ACTS has helped me. A is for adoration, meaning we should spend some time just praising God for His goodness and attributes. C leads off a time of confession, where we acknowledge our failures, bad thoughts, and deeds, and ask for forgiveness. T stands for thanksgiving! How the "attitude of

A = ADORATION

C = CONFESSION

T = THANKSGIVING

S = SUPPLICATION

gratitude" can change our perspective when we take time to give thanks. After spending some a few minutes on A.C. and T., we get to S for Supplication. Now, when our hearts are clean, our focus on God, and we are not in a greedy, selfish state of mind, we are invited to "make our requests" or "bring our petitions" before God. Yes, we can ask for things. But without the right framework, we might be asking in vain.

> *On your knees, the devil flees!"*
> —Angie Massie, missionary in Florida

THOSE AREN'T
FOOTPRINTS IN
THE SAND

One night I had a scary dream of a walk along the beach,
Pondering why my goals in life now seemed so out of reach.

Looking back upon my life, while gazing down the coast,
I noticed footprints in the sand, and what bothered me the
most

Was during the good times in my life, when things were
going fine,
There were two sets of footprints, the Savior's, and of mine.

But during times when I struggled, with depression and
defeat,
There was a single set of footprints, made by one person's
feet.

A zig-zagging pattern continued as far as I could see.
Two sets, one set, with deep grooves, quite a mystery.

The single set of footprints often turned the other way,
With two deep grooves between them, causing me to say,

"Lord, what is this I see? I want to understand.
Why is my life so filled with pain? Was any of this planned?

"When we walked together, there was joy, I must confess,
But many times I felt alone, and my life was quite a mess."

The Lord spoke rather quietly, a soft and loving tone.
"So many times you ran from Me, trying to make it on your own.

"As your Shepherd, I tried to lead you, to guide you in 'the way.'
But you, like so many of my sheep, kept going far astray.

The grooves you see are a sign of My love; they do not show My wrath.
They are the times I drug you back to the blessed path."

The Lord then said, "I only try to bless you, I hope you understand!
There is a message behind what you see,
 For they are Buttprints in the Sand."

—Gordon Douglas

219

PART IV

READY TO LAUNCH

CHAPTER 31
CAN YOU HEAR ME NOW?

"If talk is so cheap, how come I have such a big phone bill?"
—Milton Berle

"When we talk to God, we are praying. When God talks to us, we're schizophrenic!"—Lily Tomlin

"A snail makes its way across the porch and knocks on the door. A man opens the door, sees the snail, and tosses him across the yard. Three years later, the snail is on the porch, knocks on the door. When the man opens the door, the snail asks, 'Now, what was that all about?'"—Drew Carey

Can you relate to the snail? Have you ever gotten close to a goal, then experienced an unexpected setback? Ever feel like you're not sure what's going on, or had long delays? It had been over twenty years since my last show, and ten years since

223

the man prayed over me at Creation, saying I would speak to hundreds of thousands of people. I had pretty much given up on comedy. As a pastor in a Baptist church, where eternal destinies are discussed and the destinations of heaven and hell declared, I was called to live a holy life. The stereotypical Baptists in those days were somber folks in starched white shirts who never smiled. There was no card playing, movie theaters, or make-up for women, even if they needed it. And, of course, anything that could lead to dancing or associated with dancing was taboo. Safe to say that "Comedy, laughter, even giggling" wasn't very high on the priority list. That stereotype is not true for most Baptists, at least today.

And it's not true of the Amish either. I should know. I've done a few shows for the Amish community. One was for over 600 Amish dairy farmers. When I was introduced as the father of nineteen kids, one of the farmers yelled, "ROOKIE!" and the whole room erupted in laughter. And the next hour was a joy. They even invited me back next year, which is great, though strange, considering I didn't sell a single DVD that night. (Note to self: next year bring some generators!)

But here I was, working my way up from youth leader to youth pastor, associate pastor to assistant pastor. Now, pastoring my own church. A small church; a solid Bible church. This part of my dream came true. I would preach and try to be serious (no, really!), but something would always come out and folks would just burst out laughing. Still, I hadn't done a real comedy show in over twenty years. I wanted to preach and teach, not necessarily make a room full of strangers laugh.

But no matter how serious I tried to be, something would come out of my mouth and folks would laugh. A lot. One of our church members was a retired missionary from Zambia. Roberta Fine, now in her eighties, was full of joy and wisdom. One Sunday morning after another big laugh, she asked me, "Do you ever think that maybe God made you funny for a reason? Stop trying to be so serious and just be yourself. We need to laugh more!" I never saw my sense of humor as a gift from God, or a possible ministry. Could it be?

It wasn't long after that that a phone call came asking me if I still did comedy. My answer was a quick, "No! I'm a pastor now." That was followed by an even quicker click of the phone hanging up. Then, a few days later, a second call came, and then a third, all asking if I still did comedy. How strange is that?

My wife saw me hanging up the phone with a puzzled look. "Who was that?" I told her about the three calls, and she said, "This is kind of like when God called out to Samuel. Remember how he kept running to the priest, Eli, until he figured out it was GOD?" I hate it when my wife quotes the *Bible* to me. I mean, I'm the one who went to Bible college and seminary. But we did something we don't do enough— we prayed together. Right there in the kitchen, holding hands, the smell of spaghetti sauce filling the room (which

225

means it was Wednesday because we always have spaghetti on Wednesday). Though my South Philly boys wouldn't call it "sauce." They would call it "gravy."

"Lord," I prayed as I held my wife's hands, "if this is You, You have to open the doors. I don't want to get an agent. I don't want to go back to the old life, but if there's a way You could use me and comedy to build Your kingdom and share Your love, You will have to do it." To my conservative way of thinking, there was no way God would use comedy to build His kingdom. And that, I thought, was that.

Until the next day when the phone rang with another call asking me to do a comedy show. My fourth call. Apparently, I'm not as smart as Samuel. It was from someone who attended the church my wife grew up in. Connie Culley now lived in South Jersey and wanted a clean comedy show. "Oh, and since it's Christmastime, could you maybe tell the Christmas story, but in a fun way since this isn't a church show?" Wow, wow, wow! Do comedy and tell the Christmas story? That is exactly what we prayed for yesterday.

"Sure, I can do that," I quickly answered. "So, when is the show?"

"Tomorrow!"

"Tomorrow?" (Truth is, I don't remember if it was one day or one week. But I do remember there was precious little time to prepare.)

A wave of panic washed over me. Could I still do comedy

after a twenty-year break? My old dream long dead now stirred in my mind. We got a sitter for the kids and retrieved my box of jokes and routines from the attic. My wife drove to the gig, while I sat shot gun so I could go over the jokes I threw together. Speaking each joke out loud, trying to get the rhythm and remember the key words, while telling my wife how to drive is very difficult.

A good-sized crowd of several hundred folks of all ages and all races filled the firehouse. They obviously all had one thing in common—they wanted to laugh. I stood at a pool table, offering a quick "Help me, LORD" prayer, and He did. For the next hour (a whole hour!), I told stories and jokes, and folks rolled on the floor. And I knew it was GOD. I had never done a show that long before, or had so many BIG laughs. Julie DeJohn would have been proud. They even recorded it with a RadioShack cassette recorder that sat on the pool table, and I got a pretty good copy of a great show. That little cassette was about to open a door bigger than I could ever dream of.

A recent Facebook meme said, "Sometimes you need a second chance because you weren't quite ready for the first!"

Does that Facebook meme speak to you? Does it seem like life passed you by? Has your dream died? Moses thought he was ready, but spent forty years in the desert before he became Israel's deliverer. Like the snail, Moses might be asking, "Now what was all that about?"

Malcolm Gladwell wrote in his book, *Outliers,* that ten thousand hours is the magic number for greatness. Can you imagine doing anything for ten thousand hours, or even ten thousand times? Puritan theologian Jonathan Edwards talked about the process where there is a "death of a vision" that precedes its fulfillment. It sure worked out in that order for me. A dream long dead was being revived. What has changed in you or your dream over the last ten years?

CHAPTER 32
DON'T FOCUS ON
THIS FAMILY

"I grew up in a tough neighborhood. The other day, two guys were standing on the corner. One says, 'Yo, Vinny, what a shame what happened to Vito yesterday!' 'SHHHH!' Vinny replied. 'That's not till tomorrow!'"—From the Files of Tommy Moore

"I grew up in a tough neighborhood. I tell ya, the other day a guy pulled a knife on me, but I could tell he wasn't a pro. The knife had butter on it!"—Rodney Dangerfield

My kid can beat up your Honor Roll student!—Actual bumper sticker at the school in my neighborhood

"A nun asked a little boy, 'Who shot Lincoln?' And the boy answered, 'I didn't do it!' So, the nun smacked him. The next day, the boy's dad shows up demanding to know why his son was punished. The nun said, 'I asked him, 'Who shot Lincoln?'

and he said he didn't do it.' The dad said sternly, 'I've known my boy his whole life, and if he says he didn't do it, then he didn't do it!'"—Cozy Morley

My friend, Ken, sat in a chair as a crazed man held a gun to his head. Really. "Are you ready to die? Do you want me to blow your brains out?" I had prayed for Ken for years, before we even met. How? Why? I worked with his father for years at the oil refinery in South Philadelphia. Ken's dad was a pastor in training, and solid Christians at the refinery were as rare as dancing champions at a Baptist seminary. Each time his dad came to our boiler house, we would chat about the Lord and what he was studying at Bible school. He always ended with "Please pray for my son." And I did.

Years later, after being laid off, I ran in to both Ken and his dad. Ken had been what we call in the church "gloriously saved." Which means my prayers were answered, and he was no longer "testing pharmaceuticals." We had many common interests, and it didn't take long for Ken and me to become good friends. A few years later, Ken became a pastor, too! We shared a dream, and joined forces to try and help the youth in our area. This was as near to his heart as mine because he lived and worked in a rough part of town.

It was here, not far from my church, that Ken went to check on a troubled tenant in an apartment. For three hours, he was threatened with torture, and death. He claims no exceptional courage, but he did quote every verse he could remember about "spiritual warfare." Verses like, "Resist the devil and he must flee!" "Greater is He that is in you, than he (the devil) that is in the world." "Since God is for you, Nothing can be against you."

Prayers went up, God's Word went out, and drugs wore off. Calm replaced craziness, and after this three-hour showdown, my friend was told he could leave. And you know what he did? He stayed. Ken said, "How about we pray first?" The man with the gun, fearing he might be attacked if he closed his eyes, said, "You pray!" And he did.

Ken and I began meeting for prayer. One day, Ken called to tell me a new pastor who had moved into town was looking for prayer partners. Dr. Michael O'Donnell was pastoring and teaching in Texas when he and his beautiful wife, Rachel, experienced the hardest thing parents can go through. Their little daughter, Cara, had a serious brain malady, and her time on earth was cut short. Michael and Rachel needed some healing, so they moved back to our area to grieve and be with family. Soon, Michael joined Ken and me for prayer. Turns out, we went to the same high school four years apart, and were both runners.

After two or three meetings, I learned that Michael had written several books. His newest was *What a Son Needs from His Dad: How a Man Prepares His Sons for Life*, and he was going to Colorado to visit *Focus on the Family* to promote it. He wanted someone to go with him for accountability and prayer. There are a lot of dangers for men on the road, especially if you are in ministry. It helps to have someone with you. Michael had asked Ken, but Ken couldn't make it. So, this incredible door to fly to a beautiful state and visit my favorite radio ministry opened. Something amazing was about to happen.

In the hotel, we started swapping stories about stuff we did and how we got to this point in our lives. When I mentioned my love of comedy and my short but eventful career, Michael's eyes lit up. "I love comedy. Do something!" When most people hear you are a comedian, they respond with, "Tell me a joke!" Do they do that for other careers? "Oh, you're a doctor—could you look at my rash? "Oh, you're a carpenter—nail something for me!"

But there in the hotel, wearing boxers and a T-shirt (my pajamas of choice), I used a toothbrush for a microphone and did some of my old routines. Michael laughed and contributed some great jokes and a Mel Brooks impression. The next day, we went to a large chain bookstore to do a book signing. I sat in the back praying for my new friend and enjoying stories on how his book came about.

"Let me introduce you to my friend and prayer partner." I heard the words, but they didn't really register. "Gordon, come up here and share some of your comedy!"

No warning, no prep time, just go up and perform. And they

laughed. Over the next week, he did this to me at a college or two, and a few other bookstores.

His interview with *Focus on the Family* was great. What an amazing campus and tour. I was like a little kid, touring Whit's End, and watching shows get recorded. Several of the staff took us to lunch, and there in the restaurant, several tables were pushed together to allow room for our group of about twenty folks, including a few vice presidents and department heads. Michael fielded all kinds of questions about his education, research on fathers and families, and his goals for the book. He made a great impression... and then he did it again.

"Hey, guys, there's someone I want you to meet. The guy sitting quietly at the end of the table is my friend and prayer partner, Gordon Douglas, and HE IS A COMEDIAN. Gordon, share something with these folks." And I stood and did my comedy that had been tested and polished that week. And they laughed.

After lunch, one of the staff asked me what I was doing tomorrow. Why? "We're doing a conference on child abuse, and it's very heavy information. A little comedy might be needed after hearing some of the stuff that's going on."

So, the next day, I shared some of my story about taking in boys who had experienced the very things the conference was discussing, and I threw in some humor. It went great. Tickles and tragedy. Pain and punchlines. A new recipe for ministry was being birthed.

In such a short time, I went from performing in a firehouse to a Focus on the Family conference. I had done more comedy shows in a month than I had done in the last twenty-three years. That seemed impressive enough, but something even bigger was about to take place.

After lunch, Dr. David Gatewood, the head of the counseling department at that time, handed me a flier for a PK conference. PK was before Promise Keepers—it was a "Preachers Kids" conference hosted by a young female comedian named Chonda Pierce. David said, "I think you and Chonda would make a great team."

He then he asked if he could pray for me. "Sure!" I believe in prayer, but never had anyone prayed for me like this. Certainly not someone I just met. And as he prayed, his wife wrote down what he said. He spoke of things he could not possibly know about my dad, the color of Dawn's hair, and details about my brother-in-law who was born with Down syndrome and lived with us for eighteen years. He spoke as though the Lord was speaking directly to me, through him.

Some of it is too personal to share, but here is a portion of what he prayed:

Gordon, my son, you were not an accident, I formed you.

Strong father, big ideas, demanding of himself and of you.

Awkward body. Floating spirit.

Your father was perplexed with you, my son.

Mysteries of his broken body still haunt you, I KNOW!

Mysteries that we will discuss throughout eternity.

But the beauty of your spirit, and your serving him so well was the echo of my Spirit knocking at his door.

It did not go awasting, your servant's heart, my son.

It is a blessing to your wife and her brother, a child of the SON.

You know the world of the handicapped, and the ache of awkward bodies trying to fit in this world of beauty and harmony that they miss daily in their lives.

You wash the feet of any broken sheep and you serve them far and wide.

And on that I find your mercy reflects the mercy of my Son.

Tragedy and broken hearts—you know that world so well, and that is why I have given you a gift of laughter and humor that will serve my people well.

Echoes of the Fisher King, you are to me my son—the one who serves the poor and attends to them so well.

Have I not given you a palace for your home for the children that you love so well?

And a redheaded beauty, the tender queen of your domain?

Your home and your family—are they not your peaceful retreat, with noises and echoes of children at your feet?

Lazarus, my son, a beggar you seem to be, but, in fact, I have given you satisfactions AND MY SON.

Floating spirit, butterfly for my sheep, landing on their flowers and "In planting" them with love.

Love and Laughter, tragedy and pain, you are my storyteller to my sheep who are in pain.

Even as you said today, you marvel that not a bird falls to the ground without my awareness.

Then know deeply in your spirit, all your tragedies and your tears I have collected as diamonds over the years.

I will spread like stardust, humor among my people over the years.

Oscar awards will not come from Hollywood and Vine, but I will give you many Oscars in the kingdom of the Divine.

This prayer is deeply personal, but there is a message here for you, as well. I want you to be encouraged. I want you to know that God's love for you is no different than His love for me. He knows what bothers us; what struggles we face. Can you hear the passion in this prayer? Do you see the similar themes of what the man prayed for me ten years earlier? Bruce Wilkerson has a fantastic book on finding and following your dream called The Dream Giver. There is almost always a time of preparation. The basic principle is this: the bigger the dream, the longer the preparation period. When you give your dream to the Dream Giver, He gives it back to you as part of His dream for the world. And my world was about to change. What about you? Even if nothing seems to be happening, something is happening. You are being prepared, your dream is being adjusted, new people are coming into your life. This prayer, and this funny lady with dimples and a squeaky voice named Chonda, would impact my life in a big way.

"I always wanted to ask whoever put me here, THE BUILDER, "What did you want me to do? I just want a relationship with whoever built me… this all happened too fast, and it didn't happen by accident!"
—Tim Allen, star of *Last Man Standing*

CHAPTER 33
SOUTHERN FRIED
COMEDIANS

"For months I felt like a man trapped in a woman's body, and then I was born!"—Justin Fennell

"My brother got eliminated from the spelling bee. Apparently, there ain't no number eight in the word POLLINATE!"—Larry the Cable Guy

"My husband is brilliant. He is a college professor and writes murder mysteries like Ellery Queen. Should I be worried that almost every story ends up with the wife murdered and buried in the back yard?"—Chonda Pierce

"You ever try to trim your baby's fingernails wearing bifocals? That is like playing Wac-A-Mole on a teeter-totter."—Rik Roberts

Funny lines from *Southern Songs*, presented by Aaron Wilburn:

How can I miss you when you won't go away?

Sorry I made you cry, but at least your face is cleaner.

Take me out to the cornfield, honey, and I'll kiss you between the ears!

If my nose was running money, I'd blow it all on you!

I first met comedian Chonda Pierce and her husband, David, at a church in the hills of Tennessee. David was a college professor and a writer of murder mysteries. And when it came to comedy, David had quite a sense of humor himself. The Pastors Kids conference had an all-star line-up. Singer Bryan Duncan appeared by video screen, new technology then. Famed Christian counselor Steve Auterburn was there. The original redneck comedian, Justin Fennell, shared a ride with me, and would become a dear friend and mentor. The amazing Burchfield Brothers had me in awe. We all joined in, singing a new worship song introduced by Barbra Streisand of all people. It was titled *We Are Standing on Holy Ground*. And that's exactly what I was experiencing.

There was some amazing teaching on healing wounded hearts, and what it's like for pastors' kids to grow up "living in the fishbowl." Having a few kids of my own, and being a new pastor, I can tell you people have different expectations for how a pastor's kids should behave, dress, wear their hair, and so much more. Most pastors I talk to feel extra pressure for their kids to be perfect.

Chonda shared some of her comedy and part of her painful past. There were also powerful workshops walking the hurting through steps for healing. What a weekend! So much can happen in just forty-eight hours. Many lives would never be the same, including mine.

My small part in this great weekend went as good as I could have dreamed. After the conference, some of the speakers met with Chonda and her adorable mother, who is just as funny as Chonda, at a little diner. Chonda's husband shook my hand and slipped me some money all folded up, which I quickly tucked into my pocket. You have to learn that skill as a pastor in a poor church. Dear old ladies with light blue hair come up and do the secret handshake and sneak you some cash. I wonder how they learned to do that. Did they sell drugs when they were young? Where did they get those $100 bills? Who carries hundred-dollar bills? Not me. Hmmm… maybe that's why they "felt led" to help me out.

As we headed to the car, David rushed over to me. Slightly out of breath, he gasped, "Do you still have that money I gave you?" It was in my right front pocket, where I had discretely put it, trying not to be noticed. Putting it in my wallet hadn't

The one and only Chonda Pierce giving the audience a whole of laughter and enlightenment.

happened yet. In fact, I hadn't even looked at it. "I need it back!" he said a bit apologetically. So, I pulled it out and saw two $50 bills that I handed back to David feeling a bit let down. I was thrilled to be a part of this great weekend, but it was costing me money. Money that a pastor of a small parish just doesn't have. A hundred dollars would have really helped. But this was a no-paying gig. In fact, up to this time, there were almost no paying gigs. I went anywhere at any time for any price because I loved doing it and wanted to share my story.

My heart sank a little as David took the money and put it in his pocket. Both of us glanced around, making sure no one watched this deal go down. "I gave you the wrong money. This is for you!" And David handed me two $100 bills before jogging back to his car. Are you kidding me? This paid for my trip and then some! And I had been entertained, fed, and connected with some of the best folks in the Christian world.

This wonderful weekend confirmed my dream and calling, and allowed me to meet with some of the funniest folks in the Christian comedy world. It started a whole new season of life for me. My brother Scott always says, "It's not so much what you know, but who you know!" But I didn't know anyone in Christian comedy. Fortunately, I knew someone who did, and He knows how to connect folks!

I WISH I KNEW

"When I pray, coincidences happen, and when I don't, they don't!"—William Temple

Nothing less than divine circumstances got me to do a Christmas show, just before meeting a new pastor, that lead to a trip to Focus on the Family, where an opportunity to speak at a conference in Colorado fell in my lap, that opened a door to be a part of a weekend in Nashville. It was there I not only met people who could and would help me, and got to use my gifts, but learned much about healing of wounded hearts, including my own. I wish I knew how much healing I needed before I could start helping others.

> *"Never be afraid to trust an unknown future to a known God!"*
>
> —Corrie Ten Boom,
> a Holocaust survivor

CHAPTER 34
STAR SEARCH &
THE FUNNY FARM

"Ever since 911, whenever I am in an airport, I feel soooo... Mexican!"—Nazareth, a comic from the Middle East

"On some airlines, the seats are so narrow, turning the other cheek isn't a virtue, it's a necessity!"—Milton Berle

"I made a big mistake today at the supermarket. I complimented a lady on her beautiful, intricately laced dress. But it was tattoos."—Taylor Mason

"My advice for the supermarket. You have a ten items or fewer lane. Good. Now you need a 'no small talk' lane, and a "bag your own and get out' lane."—Taylor Mason

"No, my friend. We are lunatics from the hospital up the highway, psycho-ceramics, the cracked pots of mankind. Would you like me to decipher a Rorschach for you?"—Ken Kesey, *One Flew Over the Cuckoo's Nest*

I snicker sarcastically when I watch shows like *The Voice* or *America's Got Talent*, and they ask some fourteen-year-old contestant what it would mean to them if they won. "Oh, it would be a dream come true. I wanted to do this my whole life!" *Oh, SHUSH,* I think to myself. *I have underwear older than you.* Yet, I know the feeling. I, too, had a dream. Most of us do. In fact, there is a dream inside all of us. A young ventriloquist named Taylor Mason had that dream. Long before *America's Got Talent* was a show hosted by Ed McMahon called *Star Search.* And Taylor won. A dream come true for him.

For me, it was a true thrill just to do comedy again while getting to preach every week—two of the things I enjoy most. What could bring me more pleasure than that? Well, there is only one thing, and we all know what that is. Okay, maybe two. Prayer and Praise, of course.

It was a season of growth for me. Each show led to another, and another. Some big, some small, but it didn't matter to me. I was doing what I loved, and for the greatest reason in the world—to tell folks what God did in my life, and how much He loves them.

After I met Chonda Pierce, "The Queen of Clean," her career skyrocketed. She worked with Garth Brooks, traveling across the country in a big celebrity bus, and got to tour some with The Gaithers—and she still talked to me. It seems strange to me that not everyone in the church knows her yet. Chonda has since gone on to become the number-one, best-selling female comedian of all-time. More than Phyllis Diller, or Moms Mabley, or Joan Rivers. And she still talks to me.

Chonda and David Pierce had a nice piece of property outside Nashville. They use a few cabins there to help people in ministry have a little "get away." Oh, and you're going to love this. It's called "THE FUNNY FARM". Perfect.

I'm not sure how it all came to be, but Chonda let me know that some other Christian comedians were coming to The Funny Farm for a little retreat. I didn't even know there were other Christian comedians, except maybe Ken Davis or Mike Warnke. So many folks in this comedy world, Christian or not, spend a lot of time on the road, alone. It may be hard for some to understand how lonely it is on the road. It is very hard just to be yourself when everyone wants you to be funny all the time. We desperately need each other for friendship and accountability.

But how would I ever be able to afford to take a few days off and pay for a plane ticket? Having a ginormous family has many plusses, but having extra money is not one of them. There was no way I could afford to go. Meeting folks who are doing what I dream to do would really help me pursue this comedy/ministry thing as a career. It was so close, yet seemed so out of reach.

The explosion of email has connected the world. Thank you, Al Gore! And some of us began to chat and pray for each other on the Internet. What a world. Hearing of my financial plight, one of the veteran comedians, Taylor Mason, came through. Taylor is a really good ventriloquist, who sings funny songs while playing the keyboard, and does great stand-up. No wonder he was the Star Search grand champion. We had never met, other than through email. I had offered some spiritual advice and reading suggestions to him, and I got to read the brilliant comedy stuff he churned out at an amazing rate. Taylor contacted me (can you believe that?), and offered to pay my way. Something about "frequent flyer miles," which he said was, "No big deal!"

No, it was HUGE! There was no way I could have afforded it. I am forever grateful and doing my best to Pay It Forward since then. Of course, I was new to flying, and nervous. There is a lot to learn about airports and flying.

Flying from Philly to Charlotte to Nashville should be no big deal. Like many first-time flyers, I preferred a window seat. Staring out the tiny window like a four-year-old, with my knees pressed against my chest, I saw this amazing dance performed by tractors, planes, and people. Peering out over the huge wing, men fueled up the plane. The man pulled the hose back, closed the trap door, and was wiping the side of the plane when I saw the rag get sucked out of his hand, up into the engine. "That is not good," I mused, "but it's a big engine. It's probably halfway across Jersey by now. No problem... right?" Wrong.

There was a delay—a long delay—as they made sure all the pieces of the rag were out and the engine was safe. But we eventually took off, and I enjoyed the view, looking out the window at cars that looked like ants and football fields that shrunk to the size of postage stamps. An announcement was made about connecting flights. Connecting flights? What did they say? Glancing at my watch while fumbling for my ticket, I checked the time of day and the time of my next flight. This was going to be tight!

In my world of ADD, my biggest concern was what I would do for a whole hour between flights. But that hour was gone. We landed, and I ran toward my next gate, like... well, like a former football player who shall remain nameless. But I think of him every time I eat breakfast. You will think of it if you "concentrate!" (If you didn't get that joke, let me explain. The word concentrate is what is on the side of an Orange Juice container... OJ and airports...?)

I was panting and bent over after pulling a carry-on suitcase with a handle made by the Lollipop Guild in *The Wizard of Oz*. Why do they make those things so low? Are little people laughing every time it hits my heel and then wobbles for twenty steps? 'Cause folks with ADD don't slow down or stop. But that didn't help. Like Dorothy coming to a clearing in the woods and seeing the Emerald City over a field of blooming poppies, I got a great view of my Boeing 707 as it taxied out to the runway.

My heart sank. This was my BIG chance. My whole career was hanging in the balance. If I didn't get to The Funny Farm, I didn't know what was going to happen. Gasping for air, I asked the airline folks if they could hold the plane and bring it back. They didn't. "The next flight to Nashville," the woman said, "is in two hours."

Two hours? We've talked about time and my ADD. Two hours is like watching a sloth race in slow motion. Have you seen *Zootopia*?

So, now I was angry. They knew our plane was running a little late—why didn't they hold the plane? Five minutes. Is five minutes such a big deal? In two more hours, it would be dark. Feelings of failure flooded over me. "Stupid airlines, stupid fuel man, stupid luggage designers… STUPID, STUPID, STUPID!" There were tears in my eyes and a sick feeling in my stomach. Once again, my dreams were in jeopardy. Something I was involved in seemed to be collapsing in front of me.

My long legs had been cooped up for two hours, so I started walking, pulling that stupid suitcase made by stupid people through a stupid airport. "Why does this always happen to me? Why do You let this stuff happen God? Why? Why? Why?

Aren't You supposed to be in control?" I don't realize how loud I was ranting. Someone besides the Lord heard my cries of "OH, GOD!" and "MY LIFE SUCKS!" and "WHY, GOD, WHY?"

Maybe it was the anger, maybe it was the tears, maybe it was the bag I was dragging and kicking. Maybe it was that I walked out a door and reentered—I'm not sure. But all of a sudden, a lot of folks from airport security were all around me. I'm talking "hands against the wall." And guys with guns, and two guys with a blanket. A blanket? My "stupid little suitcase" was now being torn apart. This was post 9-11, where people crying out to God and wondering if life is worth living attracted attention. The blanket, I learned, was a portable privacy screen, so that folks at the bar can't tell if you are a "boxers or briefs" kind of guy when your pants are lowered. And they did get lowered. You get a very extensive physical exam. Turns out my prostate is fine, thank you very much. Sorry, TMI.

After that, the two hours passed quickly, and we all became friends. Humor can do a lot to disarm a situation like that. Eventually, I boarded a plane for Nashville without further incident. I kept my emotions in check and my spirits up as we landed at the airport and I raced toward the car rental stand. Despite the fact that it was very dark—this was a country drive and there were no streetlights—and it was long before the days of the GPS, I made it to The FUNNY FARM. Chonda's and Dave's place, not the one with padded walls. Though it was a close call as to which place I would end up. Music greeted me as I pulled up the long dirt drive. A group of maybe forty folks stood around a big bonfire, praising God and smacking chiggers. This was just like the retreat that changed my life in 1975, and it was happening all over again.

The next day, I learned that everyone had introduced themselves the day before and shared something of their journey in life. With forty folks who really like to talk, they were given two minutes each. Now, everyone had "shared" the night before but me. I was asked to do the same, but without the two-minute timer. Are you kidding me? Because my plane was late, I got to tell my story, an audition of sorts, in broad daylight, in front of the best and brightest folks in Christian comedy… with no time constraint! I was able to connect with folks who would have a great influence on my comedy and my life. And a few became my closest friends.

Maybe there was a reason my plane was delayed. Maybe that fuel man had wings under that jumpsuit and a halo under his earphones. Maybe it was the perfect time to meet the folks who would get to hear my story and be moved to help me, teach me, warn me, exhort me.

So, looking back, a man I prayed for introduced me to a pastor who was grieving the loss of a daughter, who took me to Focus on the Family, who connected me with Chonda, where Justin Fennell and I shared a ride, who then gave my cassette tape to Mike Williams, who knew a ventriloquist in

Left to right: Justin Fennell, Rik Roberts, Robert G. Lee, yours truly, and Paul Aldrich surround Kay DeKalb Smith at the CCA Conference. Great friends, and regulars at The Funny Farm.

New Jersey, who eventually got me a plane ticket to a retreat that would forever change my world.

I hope I never lose sight of one thing—all this was started with a mouse!"—Walt Disney

Don't forget where you came from, or who helped you get where you are. Maybe a thank-you call or card is in order. Let's learn from the *Pay It Forward* movie and help someone else.

Once you've been to The Funny Farm, it's all uphill from there, right?

They welcomed me, encouraged me, and allowed me to share some of my journey. They let me "open" for them, allowing me to share some of my journey and inviting me to events. This is what I've wanted all my life. One person paid my way; another person helped pastors; another person helped lonely comedians connect, and I needed all of them. One by one, this group touched the life of this one.

Paul Simon, in his song *I Am a Rock*, says:

I have no need of friendship, friendship causes pain.
It's laughter and it's loving I disdain.
I am a rock, I am an island.

Sorry, Paul Simon, not me. I have learned I need other people. Life on the road can be very hard. And comedians aren't the only people to struggle with loneliness. Perhaps that is why Alcoholics Anonymous is successful. Maybe it's the reason for the church. We need God, and we need each other. Connecting to a group of like-minded folks can be so helpful.

I hope that you don't think I am overstating the importance of friends. There are so many battles to be fought, and none of fight this fight alone!

Éomer to Aragorn (the Battle of Pelennor Fields): "Twice blessed is help unlooked for, and never was a meeting of friends so joyful," and they clasped hand in hand. "Nor indeed more timely," said Éomer. "You come none too soon, my friend. Much loss and sorrow has befallen us."

"Then lets us avenge it ere we speak of it," said Aragorn, and they rode into battle together.
—From J.R.R. Tolkien's *The Return of the King*

CHAPTER 35
REMEMBER THE ALAMO!
(OR WHY I SURRENDERED IN TEXAS)

Some of my Texas comedy buddies...

"I live in Northern Mexico, a little place called Houston, Texas."
—Bob Smiley

"Everything is bigger in Texas. Look at me! Four hundred pounds of Texas Love. I like to eat, and the other night I smelled chocolate cake downstairs. I started toward the kitchen and could smell strawberries in the hall. I started getting excited. My wife loves me and is making my favorite dessert. When I got to the kitchen, there was no cake, no strawberries... just one of those stupid scented candles. You ever want to see a grown man cry..."—Brent Reed

"During a tornado when I was a kid, my mom would make us sit in the tub in the bathroom. Apparently tornado's never think to look there."—Mike Hickman

What do you call a pony with a sore throat?
Answer: A little hoarse!
—From the Files of Tommy Moore

February 23, 1836. The Alamo, Texas. Eighteen hundred soldiers under Mexican general Santa Ana surround a small, abandoned, Catholic mission in San Antonio, Texas. About 200 Texans held out for eleven days. Famous folks like Daniel Boone, Jim Bowie, and Davey Crockett fought for as long as they could, hoping for reinforcements that never came. Unfortunately, Santa Ana's troops did, slaughtering every man, women, and child. The battle was a loss, but it was a turning point, and the cry of "Remember the Alamo" stirred the masses to take a stand and gain the ultimate victory.

The eyes of Texas are upon you. I was going to be on television with Dennis Swanberg. I heard Dennis, better known as "The Swan," do an impersonation of Jimmy Stewart on the *Focus on the Family* radio show. Dennis could take you back in time with his voice, re-creating classic characters like Barney Fife and Andy Taylor. You could relive sports events when he became Howard Cosell and/or Mohammed Ali. His repertoire of characters included everyone from Kermit the

Frog to Forrest Gump. But his best, by far, is the Reverend Billy Graham.

This was a milestone event for me. Every person I met excitedly told me of this amazing opportunity. After thirty years, I was going back on television, this time, not for me, but to use comedy to bless others. God is so good. Praises flowed from my grateful heart.

So much to do. I had bugged the studio folks with my constant calls to confirm how long I would have to be on stage, subjects they wanted me to discuss, what I should wear. Travel plans, haircut, everything was checked and double-checked. Ready or not, here I come!

Some people told me it was nerves, others said it was fear, and a few thought it was just bad timing. But when I woke up that day, I had a terrible sore throat. My flight wasn't for a few hours, so I downed every medicine known to man and prayed every healing prayer I knew, but I could barely talk. Getting desperate, I contacted a local pastor with a charismatic background to anoint me with oil and pray for me, but nothing changed.

The five-hour flight seemed to take days. I chugged hot tea and sucked on lozenges, and every hour or so, I tried softly to talk. Nothing changed, and my heart filled with dread. Once the plane landed and the rental car loaded up, it was off to the studio for rehearsal. There was a dressing room with a star and my name on it, but worry and fear had taken over.

Raspy would be too kind a word. I sounded like Marlon Brando in *The Godfather*. I met with the staff and tried to talk. It was painful for me and worse for them. The producer said, "I am sorry, Mr. Douglas, but there is no way we can put you on the air!" Grown men are not supposed to cry, at least in front of the girls. Fighting back the tears until I crossed the street to the hotel, once safely in my room, I fell to the floor and sobbed.

Once again, I blew it. I failed; I didn't come through. There were no praises, just pain. There was no thanksgiving, just complaining. I tried to curse out God, but I couldn't talk. *Very funny, Lord!* I pounded the bed in frustration, the suitcase falling to the floor, scattering a few books I had taken for the long trip.

After blowing my nose and settling down, I cleaned up the mess left by my tantrum. Picking up a book titled Absolute Surrender by a turn-of-the-century preacher named Andrew Murray, I scanned the first paragraph. "God must bring each of us to the point where He is absolutely everything, and we are absolutely nothing, the place of Absolute Surrender!"

It shouldn't matter to me if I'm performing in a prison or a palace, or whether I'm on TV or not. Not if what I'm doing is for His glory. And so, in that quiet hotel room, I got back down on my knees by the bed and offered a prayer of repentance. I cared more about my reputation and what others would say and think of me than I did about why the Lord might have me there. I confessed my sin, surrendered my life, my career, and my ministry to the Lord as best I could. I prayed, "It is Yours, Lord, to do with as you please."

Crossing the highway, I walked back to the studio to watch the taping of the show. Why not? Seeing a television show being made is still a really big deal, and Dennis was a hoot. He welcomed the studio audience and chatted with each person. There were some talented musicians there, like Terry Blackwood of the Blackwood Brothers warming up, and a great band jamming away as they set up some background stuff. As I went to take a seat in the audience, a guy with a clipboard and earphones called my name.

"Hey, Gordon, I got a new microphone. I want to try and see if we can adjust the settings for your voice." He wired me up, and I went on stage to do a little sound check. The folks in the audience smiled and clapped at this impromptu show. Folding my hands, I looked at this family in the front row and mouthed the words, "PRAY FOR ME," and they nodded excitedly.

After a few lines, the producer said, "I think we can pull this off. Let's give it a go!" Dennis sat in his big rocking chair on the front of an old country store and gave me a great introduction. The audience was wonderful, laughing at my silly stories, told in a froggy-but-funny voice. It wasn't the way I dreamed it would go. It wasn't a spot on *Johnny Carson*, getting huge laughs and getting called to the couch, but it was a TV show in the heart of Texas.

That show, I was told, aired in six states on a small cable station. Later, it was picked up in a few more states, then a few more, and a few more, and a few more. Since there were only a few episodes, it was rerun over and over to bigger and bigger audiences all across the country.

I WISH I KNEW

"In the very nature of things, in the whole relation of the creature to the Creator, in the life of Jesus as he lived it and imparts to us, humility is the very essence of holiness... It is the displacement of self, by the enthronement of God. Where God is all, and self is nothing."—Andrew Murray

I wish I knew that most of my struggles were needed to get my attention off myself and onto the Lord. When Jesus first called some professional fisherman to follow Him and become his disciples, they fished all night and caught nothing. Jesus, the carpenter, told the seasoned anglers to push out into the deep and cast their nets. Any fisherman knows that is the wrong time and wrong place to catch fish, but they obeyed, and soon their nets were full and breaking.

How many times do we try to do things with our own strength, or own way? Then the Lord has to allow us to fail, so that we will humbly call on Him. This Prayer of Absolute Surrender was one of the four biggest prayers I have ever prayed. The first came in 1975 when I prayed "LORD, SAVE ME." In the early '80s, I asked, "LORD, how can I SERVE YOU?"

When I prepared for the pastorate, I prayed, "LORD, SEARCH ME and remove anything that is not pleasing to you." And now, with a humbled heart cried out, "LORD, I SURRENDER to you. I can't do this without You."

CHAPTER 36
LINCOLN & LINKED IN

"The arguments of Stephen Douglas are as thin as a homeopathic soup made by boiling the shadow of a pigeon that starved to death."—Abraham Lincoln

The President told of a southern Illinois preacher who, in the course of his sermon, asserted that the Savior was the only perfect man who had ever appeared in this world, and that there was no record, in the Bible or elsewhere, of any perfect woman having lived upon the earth.

Whereupon there arose in the rear of the church a tired lady who said, "I know a perfect woman, and I've heard of her every day for the last six years."

"Who was she?" asked the minister.

"My husband's first wife," replied the afflicted female.
—Story relayed by soldier-turned-publisher James Grant Wilson *(1832-1914)*

"I wonder if Jesus wore a WWID bracelet?"—Paul Aldrich, member of Laugh for Life

"I am at the age where people keep asking what is on my bucket list. Number one on my list is not to kick the bucket!"—Robert G. Lee, member of Laugh for Life

Gettysburg was a small city of under 3,000 people in 1863. The beautiful woods and rolling hills surrounding the city were the stage for the largest and bloodiest battle in U.S. history. In just three days, there were more than 50,000 causalities. The Union lost just over 3,000 soldiers; the South, while harder to figure, was easily that many. A new development in military strategy was the signal corp. What an asset for the Union Army to be able to quickly communicate the number of soldiers and the direction they were heading. Soldiers like Lieutenant Aaron B. Jerome had a major impact on the outcome of that battle. Lt. Jerome was positioned in a courthouse steeple. Records of his communications show how Jerome could locate the Southern troops, and with flags and torches, warn some troops to prepare for the attack, while others moved to safer ground. Many lives were saved because of his work.

I had only met comedian Mike Williams once in person, but he had written me several times, encouraging me to use my comedy more in ministry. When he called and asked how far from Gettysburg I lived, I had no idea how significant that meeting would be. Gettysburg was a turning point in the Civil War, and it was a turning point in my life. Mike told me he was speaking there, and invited me to come and see what he does. Okay, a few hours riding through some of the prettiest parts of Pennsylvania is no big sacrifice.

Mike was in town to do a fundraising banquet for a pregnancy center, and while in the area, offered to do a show at a small church for a pastor friend of his. Mike has a lot of wisdom and

Mike Williams will help people anywhere—in this case, children in a garbage dump in Haiti.

passion, and tries to maximize all that he does for a grand purpose. He was giving me lessons in comedy, marketing and missions, and life. As he straightened my tie, he asked me if I was ready to "do ten minutes of my best stuff." Of course I was! I'd been around long enough to know the rule in comedy: always be ready to do ten minutes, and that includes being dressed for the gig. I wore a black shirt and bright red tie featuring the face of Bob the Tomato from *Veggie Tales*. As part of his introduction, I showed some of the funny products Mike sells. T-shirts that say "My body is a temple. I am not fat—I am a megachurch!" And books like *Turkey Soup for the Sarcastic Soul*, or *Men Moved to Mars When Women Started Killing the Ones on Venus*. Showing these products not only gets a big laugh, but proceeds from these items help fund Cups of Cold Water, a ministry Mike and his wife, Theresa, head up in the Dominican Republic.

The audience was kind to me as I opened the show, and the place erupted in laughter as Mike hit the stage. For the next hour, he showed funny props like Carrot Top, and did impersonations of singers like Garth Brooks and Cher. Laughs came in huge waves as Mike mixed in some fantastic stand-up and audience participation before ending with a powerful, moving story of his life. No wonder Mike has been the most booked and rebooked fundraising speaker in the country ten years in a row.

Laughter is powerful, and there is a lot to putting on a

www.*LaughForLife*.us

| Gordon Douglas | Mike Williams | Paul Aldrich | Robert G. Lee |

Putting the FUN back in FUNdraisers

615.370.4700 x 235

A charity that is more than the sum of its parts. Check out the website to find out more about the great work Laugh for Life does.

good show. But why we do it is just as important. Mike uses his comedy to raise millions of dollars every year for local pregnancy center ministries that offer help and support for those finding themselves in an unplanned or unwanted pregnancy. With lots of love and support (and no government money), these centers save lives and see families transformed. Mike knew I helped serve as the pastoral coordinator for the Delaware County Pregnancy Center, and so he encouraged me to use my story, along with my gifts in comedy, to help others. That was over ten years ago.

At one of the bloodiest battlefields in our country, where so many lives were lost, I was called to fight for life. I didn't know that every day, nearly as many babies are aborted as each side lost in the Battle of Gettysburg. Each day, every day, since the Roe v. Wade decision in 1973, more than 3,000 lives are ended.

Me holding a homemade ladder in Haiti, helping Mike Williams help others.

That's more than one million people per year, times more than forty years. Think how many people died in a war—any war— add those killed by drunk drivers in a year, then add those killed with guns, and you don't come close to these numbers. Mike started a Laugh for Life team that uses comedy to help ministries that offer real options, hope, and support. With Mike's help, I began speaking at banquets to raise money for pregnancy centers, adoption agencies, and so many other good causes. I call it "Hilarity for Charity", and it truly is comedy for a cause. I get to do what I love, and help others at the same time.

"In a world that is silent, one voice becomes powerful!"—Malala Yousafzai

There are many without a voice who need someone to speak for them. There are many good causes you can associate with. Like my buddy, TJ Foltz, who started Humankind Water to get clean, safe, drinking water to people. There are probably girls caught in sex trafficking and people who go to bed hungry right in your town. Find a cause you are passionate about and get involved.

These words first uttered in Gettysburg still ring true. "But, in a larger sense, we cannot dedicate—we cannot consecrate— we cannot hallow—this ground. The brave men, living and dead, who struggled here, have consecrated it, far above our poor power to add or detract. The world will little note, nor long remember what we say here, but it can never forget what they did here. It is for us the living, rather, to be dedicated here to the unfinished work which they who fought here have thus far so nobly advanced. It is rather for us to be here dedicated to the great task remaining before us—that from these honored dead we take increased devotion to that cause for which they here gave the last full measure of devotion—that we here highly resolve that these dead shall not have died in vain." (Excerpt from *The Gettysburg Address*)

CHAPTER 37
KIDS SAY THE DARNDEST THINGS

Art Linkletter, famous for his interviews of children, asked a little boy, "Who is the most important person in American history?" The young lad answered proudly "George Washington!" "And do you know who he was married to?" asked Art. "Yes. Miss America!"

A lady charged to the stage after the ventriloquist show was over. "I am so angry that you picked on my husband and me!" The ventriloquist began to offer a sincere apology when the woman interrupted. "I wasn't talking to you!" And pointing to the dummy, she scowled and said, "I was talking to him!" (True story!)

Ventriloquist Jeff Dunham asks the old man, Walter, "If reincarnation were true, who would you come back as? And what would you do?" Walter answered, "I would come back as my wife and LEAVE ME ALONE!"

Growing up, going to Dorney Park in Allentown, Pennsylvania, was a summer ritual. For more than a decade, we parked our Chevy station wagon under the Comet, a giant wooden rollercoaster. The speedway was behind us; the world of fun before us. Home movies captured it all, with close-ups of us grimacing as we took a spin in the Tilt-a-Whirl, stared in horror as we exited the haunted house, and held on for dear life as we bounced from side to side in the Scrambler and the Whip!

Wade is my youngest brother by eight years. His favorite ride was the "U-Drive Them" boats. A ten-foot boat with a steering wheel that resembled the one in the opening of Gilligan's Island with faces of the stars, like Mary Ann and Ginger, inside it. Five-year-old Wade could barely peer over the handle to see the front of the boat, but with intense concentration, he gripped the wheel firmly like he had to feather the boat through dangerous sea mines. He spun the wheel violently to the left and right as the boat gently made its way through the twenty-foot channel, coming close but never hitting the sides. Was Wade a future ship captain? No! The steering wheel wasn't connected to anything. It was just bolted to the dashboard and spun freely. The boat was guided by a steel track underneath, barely seen in the three feet of murky water.

We bigger kids knew better. There was no way he could get

271

off-course. We giggled as he docked the boat and exited with big smiles and sense of accomplishment. We older, wiser kids, waited in a long line to drive miniature cars that looked like '55 Chevys. They were about the size of a small tractor, with a lawnmower engine in it, but at least you had some control of the car. There was a real gas pedal and automatic brake, and a very narrow course. If you didn't steer, you banged into the heavily reinforced sides. And there were warning signs for those who liked to race: "NO RAMMING!" We waited a whole year for this ride, stood in line for half an hour, and then Murphy's Law happened. You got stuck behind a rookie driver whose foot went from gas to brake to gas to brake every five seconds. The course was set, so you couldn't get lost or make a wrong turn, but the ride could be smooth or it could be rough—very rough—depending on how fast you went and how well you stayed on course. There is a good life lesson there. And maybe a little insight into the "free will of man" as it relates to the sovereign plan of God.

Years later, the world took a deadly turn. The World Trade Center lie in ruins, and our country reeled from the surprise attack. For a time, my church had record crowds every Wednesday night for prayer meetings. The pews were also filled the first Sunday or two after that dreadful day, but in the weeks and months that followed, things went back to normal. For the vast majority of folks, nothing changed, except maybe there was a greater need to laugh. My comedy bookings increased, with more events in more and more states.

Heading back after one of my trips, I phoned home. If you don't know it, my wife has the greatest phone voice in the world. Really. She has this giggle in her voice that just makes you smile. A fellow pastor told me he calls my house just to hear her voice on the answering machine. This day, she was even more excited and happy than normal. "You won't believe what happened in church today!" she blurted out. "We had this thirteen-year-old ventriloquist in Sunday school."

"Oh? How bad was he?" I cynically retorted. Growing up in a small church, with an even smaller budget, we didn't see many folks with real talent. If my memory is accurate, anytime we had a guest singer, or watched a Christian movie, or watched the chalk talk guy, they were terrible. Maybe that's why today, we worship at The Foundry, a church that wants to reclaim the "arts," and use them to proclaim the message of God's love.

"No, he was really good!" my wife said with a little edge to her sweet voice. Sometimes she gets tired of my sarcasm. She went on to rave about his skills, how well he interacted with the audience, all while delivering a clear gospel message. She excitedly continued, "I told him about you!"

Okay, now she had my attention. I love it when she brags on me. Most men love it when their wives brag on them, and men, I am pretty sure it works both ways.

"Ryan and his dad want to meet you, maybe over lunch when you get home."

There is a fear among most performers that if I help someone, they may become better than me, and get that next booking. But knowing I would not be where I am without the host of folks mentioned in this book and an army of others not mentioned, my heart to help others succeed is just a tad greater then my fear. So, Ryan and his dad joined me for a meal, and I shared some of the things I've learned along my miraculous journey. There is a lot to learn about preparing for a show, traveling tips, and all that show-businessy stuff.

A few weeks later, I was scheduled to appear at a big pastors conference and invited Ryan to be my opening act. And he did great. Over the next few years, we did more and more shows together. When the TV show *Two and a Half Men* hit the airwaves, we had a show called *2½ Men for Jesus!* Me, Ryan, and the star of the show—Jeffrey.

By the time Ryan was in college, he and Jeffrey were doing more than a hundred shows a year. What a joy to see his career take off. Ten years later, the *Ryan and Friends Show* has grown to a cast of six characters, and Ryan is a now regular performer on Disney Cruises. Not only do I take great joy in seeing his career take off, a few times a year, I get to join him.

What an amazing journey, and not just in comedy. Dawn and I were there when Ryan and Gail pledged their love to each other at a beautiful ceremony in Lancaster, Pennsylvania. We held their daughter, Madeline, while her brother, Max, sat with his grandparents during a powerful "ordination" service confirming a call to minister. Though I have kids older than Ryan and Gail, we have become good friends, and go on regular date nights together. Our favorites are the mystery dinner theaters. I love trying to figure out "WHO DONE IT!"

At this point in the book, it should be no mystery as to what caused me the most "Growin'" and what caused me the most "PAIN." What is my secret to finding purpose, peace, and happiness in this life? I have shared my early days, when I was a young, struggling kid, about the same age as when I first met Ryan. You have followed my longing for acceptance, my need for forgiveness, and my hunger for truth. My search led me to believe the *Bible* is true, though often attacked, taken out of context, and twisted. I was guilty of doing the same things and spouting the same lies that are still so common today.

Looking back, it is clear God was already at work in my life, long before I prayed for forgiveness and asked Jesus to be my Savior. My life changed that day, but to be clear, I did not, and am still not perfect. As long as I am on this earth, in this mortal, now aging body, I struggle with temptations. Some days there are more victories than failures. Some days not.

There have been some terrible decisions, leading to pain, loss, and wasted years. There have also been some wonderful truths that have led to increased joy, peace, and victory. And I've done a few things, that resulted in real GROWTH SPURTS in my life. More of those will be featured in Volume Two of the *Things I Wish I Knew* series.

But if there is one great lesson that would sum up my journey so far, it is how Ryan closes many of his church shows. Ryan places Jeffrey on a stand. After an hour of listening to this little wisecracker, crowds fall in love with Jeffrey. They giggle as his ears wiggle, and roar with laughter as one funny line after another comes "out of his mouth." But there is a dramatic moment when Ryan removes his hand from Jeffrey's back, who then sits still, lifeless, and expressionless. What a picture of us without God in our life. But when we put our faith in Jesus, and the "Spirit of God who raised Jesus from the dead" comes into our lives, something amazing happens: a new life begins. Ryan explains this so well as he returns his hand into Jeffrey's back and brings his friend to life again. The message is simple: each of us needs God in our life. Though we are still alive, something is missing.

Blaise Pascal is often quoted as saying, "There is a God-shaped vacuum in the heart of every person, and it can never be filled by any created thing. It can only be filled by God, made known through Jesus Christ." It is a good summary of his actual quote, which is even more revealing, "What else does this craving, and this helplessness, proclaim but that there was once in man a true happiness, of which all that now remains is the empty print and trace? This he tries in vain to fill with everything around him, seeking in things that are not there the help he cannot find in those that are, though none can help, since this infinite abyss can be filled only with an infinite

*Ryan and Jeffrey—a great comedy (and
spiritual) team!*

and immutable object; in other words, by God himself."

The difference between Jeffrey and me is that Jeffrey doesn't fight over control—I do. So many times, I resist doing what the Lord calls on me to do. I ignore Him when He prompts me, and turn the other way as He tries to lead me. I want to do my own thing, but I want God's blessings, too. And that is a formula for disaster. The more control I give to the Lord, the more blessed I am. Yet, I resist giving the Lord control. Why? Do I doubt His power, or His love? The more I am convinced of God's love for me, the more I am willing to give Him control. Are you convinced?

Gordon Douglas

"An infinite God can give all of Himself to each of His children. He does not distribute Himself that each may have a part, but to each one He gives all of Himself as fully as if there were no others."—AW Tozer

More Growing and less pain is my goal for the rest of my life.

CHAPTER 38
THE HONEYMOONERS

Ralph: *I'll call her what I used to call her before we were married.*
Norton: *What's that?*
Ralph: *Little Buttercup. Wait a minute. I didn't call her that, she called "me" that. Little Buttercup.*
Norton laughs.
Ralph: *What's so funny about that, Norton?*
Norton: *You were a little cup of butter; now you're a ton of lard!*

Ralph: *A mustache makes a guy distinctive. Gives a man a sort of an air. Norton, you ought to grow one.*

Norton: *Nah, I don't need one. When you work in the sewer, you already have an air about you!*

Ralph: *You just decided for me, Alice. You just decided for me! I am going on The $64,000 Question. And do you know why? 'Cause I am an expert in one of their categories: AGGRAVATION!*

I am a bit of a romantic, but I am not good at planning. More of a spontaneous kind of guy. For me, a good time is just a moment away. It came to my attention that Dawn and I were approaching a tremendous milestone: twenty-five years of wedded bliss. The years had just blown by. Now, two days to plan is like a year to me, and of course, I wanted to do something special. So, after ten minutes of consideration, I figured why not re-create our honeymoon. I quickly arranged to surprise my wife at her work, before whisking her away to the Pocono Mountains, where we spent our first week as husband and wife. I sent my wife a funny, romantic telegram, much like the one I sent her to propose. I then waited outside her office for her to jump in the car so we could escape for a weekend. The kids were covered, and we didn't need to pack much in the way of clothes—not if the celebration took place the way I planned. And that was as far ahead as my thinking took me.

We drove the two hours to Lake Naomi, and when we got there, I couldn't believe it—the lodge was gone. The lake was still there, though a bit overgrown and a few feet shallower. A decayed canoe lay near a rotted dock. Was this a foreshadowing of something to come? No worries. There was some place to stay every fifty miles or so in the Poconos, right? After driving and driving, we spotted a truck stop. Where did the rumor that "truckers know all the good eating places" come from? We grabbed a few things to nibble on, got a blanket out of the trunk (the one we used at Little League games), and turned this into a picnic. We ate; we talked. We sat on our blanket, eighteen-wheelers pulling in and out, giving us a courtesy honk of the horn. Perhaps they saw the gleam in my eye, or perhaps it was because I told just about everyone in the truck stop this was our anniversary. To top it all off, I brought a book by Norman Wright on marriage. Norman Wright has written more than ten books on marriage, and this one had a test in it. I thought it would be fun to take a little survey to see how we were doing. I was wrong. It wasn't fun at all.

There were only twenty-five questions—apparently one for each year of our marriage. Each person had to rate their spouse on a scale of 1-10. Stuff like, "Is your spouse a good listener?" "Do they help around the house?" "Do they have a temper/ anger problem?" (See the Appendix for other questions.) I grabbed my pen and attacked the test the same way I always took tests—with the goal to finish first. Getting the right answers was secondary. I like finishing first. So, I zipped down the list, marking each line with a 10, 10, 10, and an occasional 9 to keep her humble. *This is easy, and my wife is terrific, and this should make her forget the truck stop and get her in the mood*, if you know what I mean.

Done! All twenty-five questions in less than a minute. I dropped my pencil like Eddie Murphy dropping the microphone. Glancing at my wife's paper, she was only on question five. Oh, she can be so slow and detailed, and I confess it drives me nuts sometimes, but I have learned sometimes it is best not to say anything. This was our anniversary, and not just any anniversary—it was our twenty-fifth. And that is worth celebrating. But she wasn't celebrating, she was crying. Definitely not the reaction I was hoping for.

I sneaked a closer peek at her evaluation form, and there were some 3's and 4's circled. Me? A three or four?? If you were rating looks, okay, I buy that, though in good lighting and the right haircut, I could pass for a five. With my new suit on, on a really good day, maybe a six. But as a loving husband, a romantic partner, a holy helpmate—me, the comedian, the pastor, the owner of a small business, the "father figure" to a few extra kids—how could I be a three or four? I would have asked "ARE YOU KIDDING ME?", but I could see she wasn't joking. I thought of lowering a few of her scores to an eight, but I didn't think that would help.

So, I humbled myself and asked if this was true. Through tear-filled eyes, she explained how ministry, comedy, and work had consumed me. My driven personality and desire to be liked by everyone meant that everyone else got the "Best of Gordon", while she got "leftovers." It wasn't easy to hear, but it was true. I was a shell of the husband she wanted at the end of exhausting days working two jobs, going to Bible school at night, pastoring a church, and yes, coaching several of my kids sports teams.

Honest evaluations are important to see how you are really doing, not only in marriage, but in life, and in your relationship with God. First, you have to know the truth, then you have to be willing to change. I am still not perfect, but since then, we've made it another ten years. In my eyes, I am now up to a solid seven, but you better ask Dawn.

"So, it's not going to be easy. It's going to be really hard; we're gonna have to work at this every day, but I want to do that because I want you. I want all of you, forever, every day. You and me... every day."—Nicholas Sparks, *The Notebook*

As a pastor, I have sat in on many marriage counseling sessions. When asked "on a scale of 1-10, what score would you give your marriage?", most men put between a 7 and 10. Most women put it under 5. So, expectations are different. The next question is "what one thing could be done this week to raise the score?" And most women can answer without a blink. There are lots of things to improve your marriage. Learning differing personality styles and what they respond to is very helpful. You have to learn their "LOVE LANGUAGE." You have to learn to resolve differences without saying or doing things to hurt each other.

The best advice I ever heard was maybe the simplest advice. Do something every day to make your spouse smile! That's it!

It won't fix every problem, but it can change the atmosphere and put the focus on giving, not getting, serving not self, and that will go a long way in raising the scores.

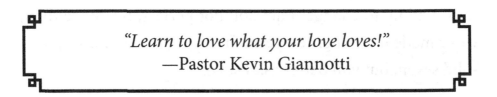

"Learn to love what your love loves!"
—Pastor Kevin Giannotti

Not married? The overriding truth of this chapter is regularly taking stock of where we are. Honest, humble assessments can be hard to take, but you can't improve your life or situation without recognizing and admitting your problems. And who knows? Finding your foibles just may lead you to find a spouse after all, or at least a better you!

CHAPTER 39
THE VOICE (WHY BLAKE SHELTON WOULDN'T PICK ME)

Yoko Ono's voice sounds like an eagle being goosed."—Ralph Novak

"You have to smell a lot of mule manure before you can sing like a hillbilly."—Hank Williams

"Sometimes we miss the humor in familiar stories. In a loud crowd, a blind man calls out to Jesus to be healed. And miracle of miracles, Jesus stops, the crowd grows silent, and the Messiah kneels down. There is a pause... and the next sound you hear is Jesus clearing His throat. 'What was going through the blind man's mind? What is He doing? Did I hear the Messiah spit? I definitely heard spitting. What is he doing? Someone talk to me? What is that wet stuff on my eyes?'"—Philly comic Al Smith

For several years, Saturday mornings were spent at the Garnet Valley gym playing basketball. Guys from my high-school team, were joined by some local dads, and a few college guys to shoot hoops. Several hours of pretty intense full-court madness. When my boys were younger, they would come to watch and run on the court to take shots between the games. Almost every week, the morning would end with some of us dads playing a game with their sons. It is one of my fondest memories. As the boys got older (and better), they often played against the men. It was heaven on earth for me.

It often got a bit rough as we grabbed instead of jumped, and relied on strength instead of speed. One game, rather than jump for a rebound, I waited to snatch it out of a Mike's hands. Mike Smitheman is a big guy with a big heart. We were teammates in high school and would later coach a team together. Sensing my attempted pilferage, he grabbed the ball with both hands and turned hard and fast, with elbows extended, just the way we were taught. I did NOT dislodge the ball, but he dislodged me. His elbow inadvertently connected with my protruding Adam's apple. Some said if I didn't have an Adam's apple, I would have no shape at all. But now, my Adam's apple was no longer protruding—it was swelling a bit, but definitely not protruding.

I stood, stunned, as play continued to the other end of the

court. As the other team dribbled the ball back toward me, one of the guys noticed the strange look on my face. "Gordon, you alright?" I tried to answer, but couldn't talk. I could barely breathe. A noise like my dog's squeaky toy came out of me. They sat me down, got me an ice pack, put in a sub, and continued to play. It's what guys do.

After the game, guys came over. "Are you okay to drive? Can I take you home?" I tried to answer, but just squeaked. So, I nodded, gave a thumbs up, and grabbed my gear and keys. Once home, I sucked on Popsicles and put more ice on my neck. Surely, this would get better in an hour or so. But, by Sunday night, it got worse. It felt like I had swallowed a box of toothpicks.

After two days, I ended up going to the doctor, who sent me to an ear, nose, and throat guy. And you won't believe his name: Douglas Gordon. Dr. Douglas Gordon Mann asked what seemed to be the problem. "I think I broke my Adam's apple!" I whispered. The trained specialist told me you can't break your Adam's apple, as it is mostly cartilage. He even took my hand and pressed it on his throat so I could see how soft and flexible it is. Then, I took his hand and put it on my throat where he could feel the "pieces of bone" and hear clicking noises.

An MRI showed that I had shattered my larynx. Those two days turned into two weeks, and then two full years. I could barely talk above a whisper. It took days for my voice to recover

287

from any attempts to preach. A few comedy shows came in, and I made it part of my act, doing *Godfather* impersonations. People still laughed, but it was hard to do more than a show a month.

Over the next two years, many cameras were sent down my throat, studies done, and vocal coaches brought in, but nothing restored my voice. It was a very dark, dark time for me. My dreams were being dashed yet again, as everything fell apart. I attended several healing conferences and was told to claim my healing. I was anointed with enough oil to lubricate a Winnebago. I read every Scripture on healing, and there are many, like "By His stripes we are healed" and "Praise the Lord, O my soul, and forget not all His benefits, Who forgives all your sins and heals all your diseases." The *Bible* is full of miraculous stories of people being healed from all kinds of afflictions. And I read many modern-day stories of people being healed of far worse things. All that just added to my guilt. "Why wasn't I healed? Doesn't God care? I know He has the power to heal, so what is wrong with me? What sin did I commit?"

I tried home remedies, and still there was no change. Was it my lack of faith? Was there some hidden sin? Was there some demon that needed to be cast out? Did I just have to accept this as God's plan?

I had read enough books on healing to know that Jesus healed everything, everywhere He went. He even raised the dead, several times. So, in my mind, it wasn't a case of CAN JESUS DO IT, it was a case of if He can, why isn't He? Was there something I needed to learn, or do, or believe? Some people told me that we are to "give thanks IN everything, that this was like Paul's thorn in the flesh that he asked God to remove three times, and yet it seemed, God said no. "My strength is perfected in your weakness!" If I never got healed, was I willing to accept this and praise God for everything else He has already done for me? Surely, He is worthy, and I recognized that I don't deserve the many blessings I have.

Did I need more faith? Some people told me I did.

I called the ministry of Joni and Friends to verify this story, and they did not find it in her books. But I remember reading or hearing this, and have been telling it for years. In my mind, I can hear her saying this after breaking her neck and spending a few years in a wheelchair. "I wanted to be healed so much that I went to a faith healer. One of those big stadiums where folks in wheelchairs come and hope for a miracle from some guy with perfect hair and teeth. At one point, the preacher points at her and says, "GET UP OUT OF THAT CHAIR!" But nothing happens. He yells, "If you had enough faith, you would get up out of that chair!"

I had been told that and my father had been told that—and it infuriates me. In my version of the story, not verified by Joni Eareckson Tada, she gets equally angry and pushes the joystick on her electric wheelchair full speed forward and rams into

289

the faith healer's shin. As he jumps up and down, holding his throbbing leg, she says, "If you had enough faith, your shin wouldn't hurt!" I love that. If it's not a true story, it should be.

I have read a lot of books on healing, and there is a lot of healing in the bestselling book of all time, the *Bible*. When God heals, how God heals, and what God heals, is amazing. God refuses to be put in a box. Like Al Smith's joke at the beginning of this chapter, there are some very unlikely people getting healed in some very unconventional ways. I'm no expert on this subject, but my favorite book and approach to praying for someone who needs healing is *Power Healing* by John Wimber. There may be something better out now, but his book lays out a great approach to finding out what God wants to do before making proclamations that can make the person feel worse if healing is delayed (or even denied for reasons we may not know). I've learned this, the more we study healing, and the more we pray for people, the more folks get healed. I am still learning.

It had been more than two years since that basketball game. It was 2007, and the Eagles were on *Monday Night Football*, a special treat for all of Philly. My wife and I put on our team Jerseys— she wears Brian Dawkins, and I have an old McDougle shirt. We wear these just in case the coach loses his mind and wants to put us in the game. My sweet, quiet redheaded bride goes through some transformation during football, yelling and screaming in ways you wouldn't believe.

Think Bill Bixby to Lou Ferrigno in *The Incredible Hulk.*

I tell the coaches what to do through the TV set. I lean as they run, trying to control the players with my mental remote control. And, yes, it is true, I have drawn up plays and sent them to the Eagles. Really!

If you think that's strange, you'll really think this is strange: my wife controls the remote. During commercials that might have something offensive to me, or my sons, she changes the station to protect our minds. During one such break where too many bikinis were on the screen (Honestly, I've seen more material in an "eye patch"), she scanned the channels and found *The 700 Club.* I signaled her to stop with this little bell I had. I also had a tablet to write down notes, so we could avoid talking. MIMES BEWARE—I was getting good at this non-verbal communication thing. It was a whole new love language for me.

There, on the screen, was a younger white guy and a woman. Not Pat Robertson, or Ben (the black preacher I saw when I last watched years before). This was Gordon, Pat's son, and former Miss America Terry Meeuwsen. They had their heads bowed and were praying. "Hmmm. Check this out," I whispered, mocking their "words of knowledge" about people in TV land with various illnesses and maladies. "Oh, somebody in Hollywood is getting a divorce," impersonating them with my froggy voice. "Somebody in construction has a bad back, or a bad knee! Whoa, what a prophet!!!" Funny stuff, right?

My boys were not amused and were anxious to get back to the game, but something happened that stopped us in our tracks. Before my wife could push the button on the remote, the woman said, "Somebody has injured their throat. There was an injury to the chords." WHAT DID SHE SAY? I can't remember everything, but there were a few details as to when their throat got hurt. "GOD IS HEALING IT NOW!" she proclaimed, and this TV couple continued on.

Forget football. My wife and kids joined me on my knees on the floor. "Please, Lord, I want to be healed. Please, please, please, let me talk again! I want to preach Your Word. I want to do comedy. You are in control of everything, and I surrender to you. Help me, Jesus."

"Is it any better?" my wife asked. I tried to talk, and do you know what happened? NOTHING!

As much as I love football, I couldn't enjoy this game. A cloud of discouragement hung over me; a wave of disappointment swept over me. It was cruel to tease me like that. If I could talk, I would have had a few words for God, but since he could read my mind, He knew I had some nasty thoughts going right then!! Walking to the kitchen, I picked up the phone and called a pastor, a charismatic Baptist who God miraculously healed after a car crash. We met at a prayer meeting in 1991, and had been praying together every Friday ever since. I couldn't cheer the Eagles on or perform as often as I liked, but yes, I could still speak loud enough to be heard on the phone.

"Hi, Pastor Tim. Yes, yes, I guess you are watching the game. Sorry to interrupt, but my wife switched on *The 700 Club*. I was making fun of it, and they said something about a guy who can't talk and broken vocal chords, and we prayed, and once again, nothing happened."

"Gordon, do you think that 'word' was for you? Think of the odds of the Eagles game going to commercial at that moment, you hit the remote, and turn to that show, where out of all the sicknesses and injuries in the world, they talk about something that sounds just like yours."

Good point.

"You need to receive it," he said confidently.

"I'm not sure what that means," I replied.

He explained that I had to have the same kind of faith as when I received the Lord into my heart. There was a point where I knew in my head that Jesus died on the Cross, and there was a point where I knew in my heart that on that cross Jesus died for me, and I needed Him. Pastor Tim closed by saying, "If you think that 'word' was for you, start thanking God for it—it's yours!"

Do you know how stupid it sounds to say, "THANK YOU GOD FOR HEALING MY VOICE" in a voice that sounds so bad? But I did, over and over, and you know what happened? NOTHING! NOTHING!!

Sinking further into despair, I went to bed. I had agreed to speak in Virginia the next day. Despite my voice problems, the Lord was using my Hilarity for Charity comedy show to raise funds for all kinds of good causes. Tomorrow would be to buy a new home for an orphanage in India. Wanting to rest up before the long drive, I was still sleeping when the phone rang. I tried to shake off the sleep and gave my best cheery "Hello!"

"Good morning. Is Gordon Douglas there?"

"Yes, you have him!" I said.

The lady said, "No, no, I want the comedian Gordon Douglas. The guy with the froggy voice. We spoke yesterday about tonight's banquet, and we want to go over some details."

"This is him," I said again, with a little surprise in my voice.

"Gordon? Gordon, is that you?" asked the event planner.

"YES, YES, YES!" I said with a voice, loud and clear. I began running through the house with the cordless phone. "I CAN TALK! I CAN TALK! I CAN TALK!!" My voice had returned 100%, and I haven't lost it since.

This dear group of missionaries had prayed through the night for this orphanage in India. She told me that between four and five in the morning, they prayed just for me!

And now, I COULD TALK!

An absolute miracle. A video of it is on YouTube. *The Comedian Who Lost His Voice.*

What happened at the banquet that night is another miracle story for another book, but the home for the orphans was purchased. Since that day, my voice is back. I can talk, I can preach, I can do comedy, and I can speak clearly without pain. And I want to use it to bring a message of love and laughter, hope and healing to this world. I still have some questions. Why did it happen in the first place? Did God cause it or allow it? I don't know. Why did it take so long? I don't know. But I do know this: I am grateful. God often does things in ways and through people we would never imagine. Including me!

I've learned the hard way that I can't do anything without God's help. I want my life to count, I want to make a difference in this world. I believe this is a plan for each of us, and finding that plan and walking the path God has for us is the biggest key to finding joy, purpose, and meaning in life. I sure don't want to miss God's best. I still wrestle with why there is so much pain in the world, and why my life has been so hard at times. People tell me "everything happens for a reason," but I don't always see the reason. But at this phase of my life, I can look back at my darkest times and see where some good has come. This book barely scratches the surface.

One of my favorite lines is "God will never make a bad thing good, but He can make something good come out of a bad thing." I've seen it happen enough that I choose to trust him in those times when I haven't gotten answers yet. The tough times have humbled me, helped me refocus, forced me to examine my heart, caused me to have more compassion for others who are hurting, and appreciate the good times.

"I would rather entertain and hope that people learned something than educate people and hope they were entertained."—Walt Disney

I hope reading this book has been entertaining and helpful, and you not only laughed but learned some key truths and principles to improve your present life and prepare you for the next! So, what's next? For me, a season of suffering and struggling had just ended. I've learned that the biggest battles often come before the biggest blessings. If the pattern holds, something really good is about to happen.

"... all we have to decide is what to do with the time that is given us."—Gandalf the Grey

CLOSING THOUGHT

The poem on the next page dates back to 1953. Its author remains unknown, but his or her words live on. This rendition features a few modifications from me. I hope the author, whoever he or she was, doesn't mind.

Lord, let me bring a little mirth to all who share my days on Earth

Let something I have said or done remain when I have traveled on

To prove the man I tried to be, and make men glad they walked with me:

A laugh or smile, a word of cheer, make these my gifts from year to year.

Lord, let me share where e're I go, some little joy to all I know.

Let these into my life be wrought: A little faith, a little thought,

A little mirth, a little grace, all to glorify this common place

Lord, let some little splendor shine, to mark this earthly course of mine.

—Sent from my wife Dawn's Uncle Bill Hamilton, found in his dad's (Grandpop Hamilton's) belongings after his passing.

RECIPES FOR SUCCESS

There are many books, dozens of speakers, and hundreds of websites that tell you how to be successful. Here are some of the key ingredients mentioned in most of them: Dreams, Desire, Action, Persistence, Resilience, Focus, Curiosity, Imagination, Teamwork, Excellence, Diligence, Vision, and Positivity. We've touched on each of these themes in one way or another. So, now that you've gotten this far, let me offer you a treat, a reward of sorts.

My girls are foodies. They love to cook almost as much as they love to eat—and they love to experiment. Success in life and success in the kitchen have some things in common. You need the right ingredients, in the right amounts, in the right order, at the right time, and at the right temperature for the meal to be spectacular. Who we share the meal with is just as important as the meal itself. I am honored that you would share so much time with me through this book.

Now, just for fun, let me share two of my favorite recipes—Yorkshire Pudding Cockaigne and Coffee Cake.

YORKSHIRE PUDDING COCKAIGNE
(*From the Joy of Cooking* by Irma S. Rombauer & Marion Rombauer Becker)

Have all ingredients at 75 degrees. Stir into a bowl:
  7/8 cup flour
  1/2 tsp salt

Make a well in the center, into which pour:
  1/2 cup milk
  1/2 cup water

Stir in the liquid. Beat until fluffy and add 2 eggs.

Continue beating until large bubbles rise to the surface. Let stand covered and refrigerated at least one hour. Beat again after bringing it back to 75 degrees.

Preheat oven to 400 degrees.

Have ready a hot, ovenproof dish about 9x13 inches containing about 1/4 cup hot beef drippings or melted butter. Pour in the batter. It should be about 1/2 inch high. Bake the pudding 20 minutes. Reduce heat to 350 degrees and bake 10-15 minutes longer. Serve at once. (Servings: Six 3-inch squares.)

COFFEE CAKE

Mix until crumbly:
  1 cup brown sugar
  3/4 cup white sugar
  2½ cups flour
  1 teaspoon salt
  1 teaspoon nutmeg
  3/4 cup oil

Remove 1/4 of mixture for topping and place in another bowl

Add:
  2 teaspoons of cinnamon
  1 tablespoon of oil
  (Nuts can be added if you desire – walnuts work well)

Set aside. Add to the cake mix (3/4 of the mixture still in original bowl):
  1 egg
  1 cup sour milk

Note: If you do not have sour milk, combine:
  1/8 cup vinegar or lemon juice
  7/8 cup milk
  1 teaspoon of baking soda

Make sure to use a 4-cup measuring cup as the mixture expands!!!!!!!!!!

Place cake mix in a 13x9 greased and floured pan.
Crumble the topping evenly over the cake mix.

Bake in a 350-degree oven for 30 minutes.

APPENDIX

CHAPTER 21

I AM

ALIEN TO THIS WORLD	1 PETER 2:11
BORN OF GOD	I JOHN 5:18
BRANCH (OF THE TRUE VINE)	JOHN 15:1,5
CHILD OF GOD	JOHN 1:2, ROMANS 8:16; I JOHN 3:1,2
CHOSEN OF GOD	COLOSSIANS 3:12; I THESSALONIANS 1:4
CHOSEN RACE	I PETER 2:9,10
CHOSEN TO BEAR HIS FRUIT	JOHN 15:16
CHRIST'S FRIEND	JOHN 15:15
CITIZEN OF HEAVEN	PHILLIPIANS 3:20
DEARLY LOVED	COLOSSIANS 3:12; I THESSALONIANS 1:4
ENEMY OF THE DEVIL	1 PETER 5:8
ENSLAVED TO GOD	ROMANS 6;22

EXPRESSION OF THE LIFE OF CHRIST	COLOSSIANS 3:4
FELLOW CITIZEN	EPHESIANS 2:19
GOD'S WORKMANSHIP	EPHESIANS 2;10
HEIR OF GOD	GALATIANS 4:6,7
HIDDEN WITH CHRIST IN GOD	COLOSSIANS 3:3
HOLY	EPHESIANS 4:24; COLOSSIANS 3:12
HOLY NATION	I PETER 2:9,10
JOINED TO THE LORD	I CORINTHIANS 6:17
JOINT HEIR WITH CHRIST	ROMANS 8:17
LIGHT OF THE WORLD	MATTHEW 5:14
LIVING STONE	I PETER 2;5
MEMBER OF CHRIST'S BODY	I CORINTHIANS 12:27
NEW CREATION	I CORINTHIANS 5:17
PARTAKER OF A HEAVENLY CALLING	HEBREWS 3:1
PARTAKER OF CHRIST	HEBREWS 3:14
PEOPLE FOR GOD'S OWN POSSESSION	I PETER 2:9,10
PRISONER OF CHRIST	EPHESIANS 3:1; 4:1
RECONCILED TO GOD	II CORINTHIANS 5:18-19
RIGHTEOUS	EPHESIANS 4:24
ROYAL PRIESTHOOD	I PETER 2:9,10

SAINT	EPHESIANS 1:1; I CORINTHIANS 1:2; PHILLIPIANS 1:1; COLOSSIANS 1:2
SALT OF THE EARTH	MATTHEW 5:13
SLAVE OF RIGHTEOUSNESS	ROMANS 6:18
STRANGER TO THIS WORLD	1 PETER 2:11
SON OF GOD	ROMANS 8:14,15; GALATIANS 3:26, 4:6
SON OF LIGHT	I THESSALONIANS 5:5
TEMPLE OF GOD	I CORINTHIANS 3:16; 6:19
WHAT I AM	I CORINTHIANS 15:10

I HAVE/I HAVE BEEN

ADOPTED	EPHESIANS 1:5
ANOINTED	II CORINTHIANS 1:21
APPROACH GOD WITH BOLDNESS, FREEDOM, AND CONFIDENCE	EPHESIANS 3:12
BLESSED WITH EVERY SPIRITUAL BLESSING	EPHESIANS 1:3

BURIED, RAISED, AND MAKE ALIVE WITH CHRIST	COLOSSIANS 2:12,13
CALLED	II TIMOTHY 1:9; TITUS 3:5
CHOSEN IN CHRIST	EPHESIANS 1:4
CHRIST HIMSELF IN ME	COLOSSIANS 1:27
CRUCIFIED WITH CHRIST	GALATIANS 2:20
DELIVERED FROM DOMAIN OF DARKNESS	COLOSSIANS 1:13
DIED TO SELF	II CORINTHIANS 5:14,15
DIED TO SIN'S POWER IN MY LIFE	ROMANS 6:1-5
DIED WITH CHRIST	ROMANS 6:1-5
DIRECT ACCESS TO GOD THROUGH THE SPIRIT	EPHESIANS 2:18
ESTABLISHED	II CORINTHIANS 1:21
FIRMLY ROOTED IN CHRIST	COLOSSIANS 2:7
FORGIVEN	EPHESIANS 1:7,8; COLOSSIANS 1:14
FREE FOREVER FROM CONDEMNATION	ROMANS 8:1
GIVEN A SPIRIT OF POWER, LOVE, AND SELF-DISCIPLINE	II TIMOTHY 1:7
GIVEN EXCEEDINGLY GREAT ND PRECIOUS PROMISES BY GOD	II PETER 1:4
GIVEN THE HOLY SPIRIT AS A PLEDGE	EPHESIANS 1:13,14

GIVEN THE MIND OF CHRIST	I CORINTHIANS 2:16
GRACE	HEBREWS 4:16
JUSTIFIED	ROMANS 5:1
MADE ALIVE TOGETHER WITH CHRIST	EPHESIANS 2:5
MADE COMPLETE IN CHRIST	COLOSSIANS 2:10
MADE RIGHTEOUS	II CORINTHIANS 5:21
MERCY	HEBREWS 4:16
PLACED INTO CHRIST BY GOD	I CORINTHIANS 1:30
PREDESTINED TO ADOPTION AS A SON	EPHESIANS 1:5
RAISED UP WITH CHRIST	COLOSSIANS 3:1-4
RAISED UP AND SEATED WITH CHRIST IN HEAVEN	EPHESIANS 2:6
RECIPIENT OF HIS LAVISH GRACE	EPHESIANS 1:7,8
REDEEMED	EPHESIANS 1:7,8; COLOSSIANS 1:14
RIGHT TO COME BOLDLY BEFORE THE THRONE OF GOD	HEBREWS 4:16
RECEIVED THE SPIRIT OF GOD	I CORINTHIANS 2:12
SANCTIFIED	HEBREWS 2:11
SAVED	II TIMOTHY 1:9; TITUS 3:5

SEALED BY GOD	II CORINTHIANS 1:21
SPIRITUALLY CIRCUMCISED	COLOSSIANS 2:11
TRANSFERRED TO THE KINGDOM OF CHRIST	COLOSSIANS 1:13

(My wife and I spent a year reading these out loud every morning. Each one has a profound truth and benefit to it.)

CHAPTER 21

CONFIRMING YOUR CALLING

Here is a tool that I often refer to when people ask me how to find God's Will for their lives. Use the letters C-A-L-L-I-N-G.

C = Commit your way to God

Psalm 37: 4-5   Mark 14: 36   James 4: 7-10

****You will not surrender to a GOD you don't trust. The more you LOVE, the more you trust!

A = Assess your interests and talents

What do you do well? What do you like to do? Have you ever taken a personality profile assessment? They are great at finding out how you are uniquely wired. There are some free ones online if you search "Personality Assessment" or "DISC".

www.mrcmv.org has a short, free version to get you started. www.TheFlagPage.com has a more detailed version for $25.

Eph 2: 10   Jer. 1: 4-10   Psalm 139: 14   Exodus 35: 30-35

L = Learn about that career

What is involved? What knowledge and abilities are needed? Grow. Nobody starts off as a master at anything...

Matt. 11:29,   Luke 2: 52,   Heb. 5: 12

L = Listen to leaders

Ask people you trust about the kind of career that might interest you.

Prov. 1: 5   Acts 13: 3

I = Invitations

What doors are opening? What do people ask you to do?

I Cor. 16: 9, Acts 14: 27, Romans 8: 28

N = Needs

What needs do you see? We often see the world through our gifts.

Matt. 9: 36   Mark 6: 34

G = Gifts of the Holy GHOST!!

Maybe even more important than a personality profile, a spiritual gift assessment can reveal areas of strength. Here are some free ones online: gifts.churchgrowth.org, gifts-tests.com, or spiritualgiftstest.com. And here is one from The Rock Church: sdrock.com/giftstest.

When you work through the steps above, you should have a much clearer idea about which way to go, what to study, and preparation to pursue.

For Chapter 22

25 Cent Mate

Here is a fun game we used in our youth group to get guys and girls to start thinking about what to look for in a guy or girl, and to do a little self-inspection on the kind of person we are.

This section costs six cents each:
(Circle and then total each section)
- Good-looking
- Popular
- Intelligent
- A great Christian
- Kind

Each of these cost five cents:
- Good conversationalist
- Tactful
- Good manners
- Sense of humor
- Good job

Each of these costs four cents:
- Controls their temper and tongue
- Great body
- Athletic
- Attends church
- Honest

Each of these costs three cents:

- Nicely dressed/well-groomed
- Likes music and art
- Ambitious and hardworking

Each of these costs two cents:
- Tall or the right height
- Intelligent (Got or gets good grades)
- Likes children and wants kids someday-
- Brave/stands up for others

Each of these costs one cent:
- Right Hair and eye color
- Owns a car
- Good with money
- Serious

Chapter 22   Questions to Ask Before Getting Married

What you don't know can hurt you. So, if you're thinking of getting married, I suggest getting my video *Things I Wish I Knew Before I Said "I Do!"* for a fun introduction to marriage. Mark Gunger has a course title, *Laugh Your Way to a Better Marriage*, that takes it a few steps further. Here are fourteen questions that you should have answers to before you get engaged.

1. What are you and your family like when you get mad? What is your future spouse and his family like when they get mad? How do you express anger? Are you verbal, violent, or do you clam up?

2. How many children do you want? How soon? Who changes the diapers? Are there already children in the picture? Are their ex's in the picture?

3. How important is religion to you or them? Do you regularly worship? How will you raise the children?

4. Are you (or they) in debt? Who is responsible for that debt? Are they good with money? How much would you be willing to spend on a house/apartment, a car, a couch, or clothes? In other words, do you have a budget? Money is one of the top three reasons couples split.

5. How much time and money will you spend on vacation or recreation? Hunting, fishing, cruises, day trips…

6. Do you like each other's families? How much time will you spend with them? How will holidays be handled?

7. How important is SEX to you/them? How often will you have sex? How important is meeting their needs to you? How important is non-sexual touch to you? Is pornography acceptable?

8. Do you know your partners Love Language? One of the best resources is Gary Chapman's 1992 book, *The Five Love Languages.*

9. Can you list five of your partner's strengths? Five weaknesses

or pet peeves? Can you live knowing that they will probably never change?

10. Most couples never see beyond the wedding day, but where do you see yourself in ten or twenty years? There are seasons of marriage. Everyone loves the honeymoon stage, but 99% of marriage comes after that day!

11. Will you both work? How long? What shifts? Are weekends involved? If you or your spouse is offered a job in another state, would you be willing to move?

12. How much time will you spend apart versus together? Will you eat meals together? Who will cook? Clean up afterward?

13. Warning signs! Are there potential dangers habits or lifestyles that involve drinking, drugs, smoking, or hobbies?

14. What kind of friends do they have? Do you like them? How much time will you be spending with them?

Norman Wright's *Premarital Counseling* is a classic that looks at these issues and so much more! Gary Smalley's *As Long As We Both Shall Live* has a list of seventy-five expectations people have for a relationship. Like the list above, each has the potential to explode if the expectation is not realistic or discussed. Do you see any dealbreakers in the list above? Then please wait and work on solutions, or walk away.

Chapter 29   Questions to Get You Closer to God

King David, in Psalm 139, prayed, "Search me, O God, and know my heart. Try me and know my anxious thoughts." My good friend, Jim Anderton, heads up Hand to the Plow Ministries. He introduced me to some of the greatest revival principles and teachers and gave us a tool for examining our hearts so that we can be as close to God as possible. Here are a few questions off that list. Take some time, find a quiet place, and prayerfully consider these questions. If you're like me, you'll be humbled and amazed at how much junk comes into our life.

• How many times have you been blessed and never thanked God?
• How often do you express your love to God and others?
• The *Bible*, the Word of God, is one of our greatest gifts-- how often do you read it, or do you neglect it?
• Are there times when you sensed the Lord leading you to do something or say something and you let fear of what someone might think hold you back?
• When was the last time you used your tongue to lie, or curse, or gossip about someone, instead of speaking truth in love, or using your tongue to praise the LORD or just not speak at all?
• Knowing we have unlimited access to come before the

Lord at any time, how often do you pray? When you pray, how often do you just ask for things verses interceding for others?

• There are needy folks all around us. How moved are you by the plight of the poor, or are you burdened by all for the hurting?

A good prayer is "Lord, create in me a clean heart and renew a right spirit within me. Remove whatever does not belong. I give you permission to change my heart. Help me to love You and others better!"

Chapter 29   Steps to Forgiveness

Forgiveness may be one of the hardest things I've ever done, but the most freeing! Someone said "Not forgiving is like drinking poison and expecting the person who hurt us to suffer." The three best books that helped me through the process of forgiveness are *The Bondage Breaker* and *Victory Over the Darkness* by Neil T. Anderson, and *The Gift of Forgiveness* by Charles Stanley. Both authors explain what forgives is and is not. For instance, Forgiveness is not forgetting. Forgiveness is not saying what the person did to us was okay. Forgiveness is not being a doormat and allowing someone to continue hurting you physically or emotionally. Forgiveness does not seek revenge, but trusts that God will work it out in the end. Forgiveness does not deny the wrong done or the pain that you feel. It is giving up your right to be angry.

Here are just a few of the steps that these books walked me through:

- Ask the Lord to reveal who I need to forgive. The Lord is gracious and usually only a few will come to mind.
- Acknowledge the hurt. "Lord, _____ hurt me when they did _____ to me!"
- Make a conscious choice to forgive. Pray specifically. I'd even suggest out loud. "Lord, I forgive (their name) for (all the offenses done to you or things that should have been done and weren't)." Do NOT say, "I want to forgive," or "Help me forgive." You must choose to let this go!
- Do your best NOT to bring it up again. When the thought comes, and it will, say out loud, "I have chosen to forgive (name) for that (offense). I trust the Lord will now handle it."
- Ask the Lord to replace the anger and bitterness with love and blessing.

Chapter 33

Laughing in the Dark: A Comedian's Journey Through Depression by Chonda Pierce

This book has a very honest, open look at one woman's battle with depression. Not only does her humor help us through the painful process, but there are helpful questions and advice from experts at the end of each chapter.

Chapter 38

Marriage Evaluation

There are a ton of marriage assessments on the web. Some done by psychologists, some done by ministries. I like *focusonthefamily.com/marriage/promos/focus-on-marriage-assessment.*

Most assessments have questions like these:

Communication

If your spouse is a good listener, they get a 10. If your spouse doesn't listen, or interrupts, or doesn't understand, they get a

1. How well does your spouse listen? _____

Conflict (pick one that fits best)

• We argue or fight: once a month, once a week, once a day, once an hour.
• When we fight, we usually: come to an agreement, avoid conflict, get very angry (even hostile).

Caring

My spouse says and shows affection in different ways would be a 10. My spouse takes me for granted and never expresses love or appreciation is a 1. My spouse is a _____

Chores

We have clearly defined roles as to who cooks, cleans, does the laundry, takes care of the house/yard is a 10. I feel like I have to work all day, and then come home and work a second job is a 1. Your role in doing chores is a ____?

Cash

Money is one of the top three reasons couples separate.

We don't spend money we don't have, we pay bills on time,

and we don't have debt other than our house or cars is a 10. We are always behind in our bills, and have more than $10,000 on our credit cards is a 1. Your score is a _____?

Children

How many children do you want? How soon should you start having them? How will you discipline them? Do blended families add a whole new layer of potential problems? You get a 10 if you agree on these issues; a 1 if you constantly fight over how to handle the children.

How do you score?

Companionship

We have fun doing things together and regularly engage in activities we both enjoy is a 10. We never do anything together anymore is a 1. Where are you? _____

These are sample questions from several good assessment tools. You not only need to identify areas of struggle, but be ready to take steps to improve if you are below a five in any area. It takes work, but it's worth it.

Personality Profiles

One of the best things I ever learned is how differently we are wired. This is not a right or wrong test. Some folks enjoy people; some like solitude. Some are passive; some are aggressive. Some are detailed; some are more carefree. Some are loud; others are quiet. Many times these opposites attract. Each personality has a list of strengths and interests, and a list of weaknesses. It made a huge improvement in my life when I understood why I was drawn to different things, and when I understood how differently my wife and children were. It also relates to the kind of career we are best suited for.

There are some free ones online if you search "Personality Assessment" or "DISC"

www.mrcmv.org has a short, free version to get you started. www.TheFlagPage.com has a more detailed version for $25.

Or you can buy a book online for under $10 that not only has a test in it, but explains the different personality tests in great detail—their strengths and weaknesses and types of questions to expect. My two favorites are *Understanding the Male Temperament* by Tim LaHaye, and *Personality Plus* by Florence Littauer. They are fun, easy reads that have had a big impact on my life.

MY FAVORITE BOOKS

THE FINAL QUEST trilogy by Rick Joyner, Morningstar Publications. Nothing has touched my heart more in the last twenty years than this series. It's kind of a modern-day *The Pilgrim's Progress*.

THE DREAM GIVER by Bruce Wilkinson, Multnomah Press. This is fantastic for anyone looking to rediscover their dream and make it a reality.

A PH.D. IN HAPPINESS FROM THE GREAT COMEDIANS by Tommy Moore, iUniverse Inc. Old-time comedians, stories of early entertainment, and some great jokes offer a few lessons on happiness. This is a modern-day classic.

THE KNOWLEDGE OF THE HOLY by A.W. Tozer, Harper SanFrancisco and **KNOWING GOD** by J.I. PACKER, Intervarsity Press, are two classics on what God is really like. To paraphrase the hit 1958 song by The Teddy Bears, "To know

Him is to love Him."

UNDERSTANDING THE MALE TEMPERAMENT by Tim LaHaye, Baker Books. This book was eye-opening for me in understanding myself, my wife, my kids, and my friends.

THEY FOUND THE SECRET by V. Raymond Edman, published by Zondervan, is a great collection of mini biographies of twenty folks whose lives changed this world.

THIS PRESENT DARKNESS by Frank Peretti, Crossway Books. This is the only book in the last thirty years I stayed up all night to read in one sitting. A novel that pictures the unseen world of angels and demons and what affects them.

ABSOLUTE SURRENDER by Andrew Murray, Wilder Publications. A classic on the deeper life.

POWER HEALING by John Wimber, HarperOne, is my favorite book on healing. It offers great examples of miracles happening today, and serves as a step-by-step guide in how to pray for the sick.

GORDON DOUGLAS

If this book has helped you or encouraged you in any way, Gordon would love to hear about it. Please email him at gordoncomedy@gmail.com.

His website has videos of him in action, with three DVDs available for purchase. Their titles are:

Laugh All Night
Things I Wish I Knew Before I Said "I DO!"
Road to Happiness

Find them all at GordonDouglasIsFunny.com

And for a daily dose of fun and faith, look at and like...
Comedian Gordon Douglas on Facebook!

COMING ATTRACTIONS!

THINGS I WISH I KNEW, VOLUME TWO is already in the works.

More insight!
More action!
More romance!
(Oh, there's definitely more romance!)

Get the inside scoop on "How I Got Hurt at a Healing Conference!", "How to Have Fun at a Funeral", "Operation Bellylaughs", and "The Sub That Saved My Life", and (Spoiler alert!!) how my oldest daughter, Sandy, married Pastor Tim's son and blessed us with some amazing grandsons.

All that and so much more coming soon!